FOOT...
FO...
RIV...

ASTON VILLA
VS
BIRMINGHAM
CITY

Classic
MIDLAND
Derby Games

© Haynes Publishing, 2013

The right of Ralph Ellis to be identified as the author of this Work has been asserted by him in accordance with the Copyright, Designs & Patents Act 1988.

First published in 2013

A catalogue record for this book is available from the British Library

ISBN: 978-0-85733-206-6

Published by Haynes Publishing, Sparkford, Yeovil,
Somerset BA22 7JJ, UK
Tel: 01963 442030 Fax: 01963 440001
Int. tel: +44 1963 442030 Int. fax: +44 1963 440001
E-mail: sales@haynes.co.uk
Website: www.haynes.co.uk

Haynes North America Inc., 861 Lawrence Drive, Newbury Park, California 91320, USA

Images © Mirrorpix

Creative Director: Kevin Gardner
Designed for Haynes by BrainWave

Printed and bound in the US

FOOTBALL was
FOOTBALL
RIVALS

ASTON VILLA
VS
BIRMINGHAM
CITY

Classic
MIDLAND
Derby Games

Ralph Ellis

CONTENTS

Introduction

There's a thin line between love and hate, according to the old song. Those words are never truer than when it comes to football.

In every big city in Europe which boasts more than one top club there is bitter rivalry between the two teams and their supporters. Be it Celtic and Rangers in Glasgow, Real and Atlético in Madrid, or Inter and AC Milan; the one fixture that gets everybody excited is when they clash.

In England the city of Birmingham is no different. Aston Villa were formed in 1874, Birmingham City a year later, and the two have been at odds ever since. In fact the very first time they played each other there was argument. The exact details of the controversy are lost in the mists of time, but history records the first fixture in September 1879 as having been won by Birmingham "by a goal and a disputed goal to nil".

Supporters of both clubs pour scorn on those from just down the road, but can't wait for the next time they play each other. At different times in history Villa fans have cheered when Blues were relegated, and the terraces at St Andrew's have rejoiced in hearing that Aston Villa have gone down. But in the seasons when they have not faced each other, there is always something missing.

Going through the 120 competitive meetings brings repeated themes: conflict between players and supporters; tough tackles and referees trying to keep control; goalkeeping mistakes, from a Cyril Spiers own goal in the 1920s, to England star Harry Hibbs unexpectedly dropping shots over his line in the 1930s, and on to Peter Enckelman's bizarre own goal in 2002.

These are the stories of two great football clubs who can't live together, but can't thrive without each other either . . .

Honours:

Aston Villa:

Premier League winners: 0

Premier League runners-up: 1(1992—93)

First Division winners: 7

(1893—94, 1895—96, 1896—97, 1898—99, 1899—1900, 1909—10, 1980—81)

First Division runners-up: 9

(1888—89, 1902—03, 1907—08, 1910—11, 1912—13, 1913—14, 1930—31, 1932—33, 1989—90)

Second Division winners: 2

(1937—38, 1959—60)

Second Division runners-up: 2

(1974—75, 1987—88)

Third Division winners: 1

(1971—72)

FA Cup winners: 7

(1887, 1895, 1897, 1905, 1913, 1920, 1957)

FA Cup runners-up: 3

(1892, 1924, 2000)

Football League Cup winners: 5

(1961, 1975, 1977, 1994, 1996)

Football League Cup runners-up: 3

(1963, 1971, 2010)

European Cup winners: 1

(1981—82)

UEFA Cup winners: 0

European Super Cup winners: 1

(1982—83)

Fairs Cup winners: 0

Birmingham:

Premier League winners: 0

Premier League runners-up: 0

Football League first tier winners: 0

Football League first tier runners-up: 0

Football League second tier winners: 4
(1892—93, 1920—21, 1947—48, 1954—55)

Football League second tier runners-up: 5
(1893—94, 1900—01, 1902—03, 1971—72, 1984—85)

Football League third tier winners: 1
(1994—95)

Football League third tier runners-up: 1
(1991—92)

FA Cup winners: 0

FA Cup runners-up: 2
(1931, 1956)

Football League Cup winners: 2
(1963, 2011)

Football League Cup runners-up: 1
(2001)

European Cup winners: 0

UEFA Cup winners: 0

European Super Cup winners: 0

Fairs Cup winners: 0

Fairs Cup runners-up: 2
(1958—60, 1960—61)

Head to Head:

League	P	W	D	L	F	A
Aston Villa:	110	44	29	37	172	151
Birmingham:	110	37	29	44	151	172

FA Cup						
Aston Villa:	3	2	1	0	5	0
Birmingham:	3	0	1	2	0	5

League Cup						
Aston Villa:	7	4	1	2	11	5
Birmingham:	7	2	1	4	5	11

Totals						
Aston Villa:	120	50	31	39	188	156
Birmingham:	120	39	31	50	156	188

Derby Stars:

Player	Club	Years	Appearances
Joe Bradford	Birmingham	1920—1935	23
Billy Walker	Aston Villa	1919—1934	22
Tommy Mort	Aston Villa	1921—1935	19
Dicky York	Aston Villa	1919—1931	18
Stan Lynn	Aston Villa (7)	1950—1961	
	Birmingham (10)	1961—1966	17
Arthur Dorrell	Aston Villa	1919—1930	17
Charlie Aitken	Aston Villa	1960—1976	16
Harry Hibbs	Birmingham	1924—1940	15
Dennis Mortimer	Aston Villa	1975—1985	14
Eric Houghton	Aston Villa	1929—1947	14
Dan Tremelling	Birmingham	1919—1932	14
Ron Wylie	Aston Villa (10)	1958—1965	
	Birmingham (4)	1965—1970	14
Gordon Cowans	Aston Villa	1975—1985	
		1988—1992	
		1993—1994	14
Nat Robinson	Birmingham	1898—1910	13
Malcolm Beard	Birmingham	1957—1971	13
Allan Evans	Aston Villa	1977—1989	13
Des Bremner	Aston Villa (8)	1979—1985	
	Birmingham (5)	1985—1989	13
Billy George	Aston Villa	1897—1911	12
Gil Merrick	Birmingham	1946—1960	11
Billy Garraty	Aston Villa	1897—1908	11

Chapter One

The 19th Century

The beginnings were simple – two groups of lads who went to the same church and decided to form a football team. None of them could have imagined how it would turn out.

In Aston Villa's case it was the members of Villa Cross Wesleyan Chapel, who in 1874 felt it would be a good idea to create some form of organized recreation to keep healthy minds in healthy bodies. Across town the congregation of Holy Church in Bordesley Green already ran a cricket club with the same objective. In September 1875, as the long shadows of a coming autumn brought their season to a close, they agreed to start a football team with the aim of staying fit during the winter.

Nearly a century and a half later it's hard to equate such humble beginnings with the two giant clubs which dominate the sporting landscape in the modern city of Birmingham. What started as a friendly rivalry – Blues' first match was against supporters of Aston Villa – has grown into a tense, passionate, exciting but sometimes bitter contest for the upper hand.

It was Aston Villa who were quickest to establish themselves as one of the major clubs at a time when English football was in its infancy. By chance a Scotsman, George Ramsay, happened upon a group of their players practising in Aston Park and when he joined in they were so struck by his skills that they insisted he should join their team as captain – and it was he who laid down the style of the club's play to be short, quick passing.

In 1876 the club established its first proper home in Perry Barr, where up to 27,000 people could pay to watch games that were growing rapidly in popularity – and three years later they were ready for their next big step – entering the FA Cup for the first time. Remarkably, after reaching the third round and being drawn against three-times finalists and 1874 winners Oxford University, they scratched from the competition. Nobody knows why – although the guess is that they chose to concentrate on winning the Birmingham Senior Cup with a 3-1 win over Saltley College in the final at Aston Lower Grounds.

Over the next few years Villa's status grew rapidly and in 1887 Archie Hunter became the first club captain to lift the FA Cup, scoring one of the goals as the team beat West Bromwich Albion 2-0 at Kennington Oval. But if that seemed like a significant moment, then it was nothing compared to the contribution that was about to be made to football history.

William McGregor, a Scotsman who had moved from Perth to open a drapery business in Birmingham, had become involved with the club three years after it had been created. Inspired by the club's connection to a Wesleyan chapel, he began by helping to officiate in matches and eventually was invited to become a director and take responsibility for organizing the team.

Frustrated by the difficulty of arranging friendly matches, he wrote to other clubs suggesting they form a competition which would guarantee home and away fixtures. A meeting was held where his idea was enthusiastically adopted, and so in 1888 the Football League was born. The season had actually started before it was decided to award two points for a win and one for a draw as a way of settling who was best. By the end of the campaign Preston North End had been crowned the inaugural champions of the 12 clubs who took part, with Aston Villa placed second.

McGregor was appointed as the first chairman of the League, but had to wait until 1894 to see his beloved Aston Villa side win the competition for the first time. By now expanded to 16 clubs, Villa won 19 of their games and centre-forward Will Devey scored 20 goals.

It proved the start of a glorious era for Villa. By the turn of the century they had won four more titles and the FA Cup three times – including doing "the Double" in 1897, and from humble beginnings were established as one of England's leading football clubs. Encouraged by their success, and with the number of people wanting to watch their games growing rapidly, McGregor oversaw the development of part of Aston Lower Grounds, in the estate of Jacobean stately home Aston Hall, into a modern new arena with the football pitch surrounded by a 20ft-wide cycling track.

Meanwhile the club we now know as Birmingham City had actually begun life under the name Small Heath Alliance. Their first match was against a group of Aston Villa supporters, on a strip of waste ground in Bordesley Green. By the summer of 1876 they moved to a fenced-off field in Sparkbrook. The public were charged an entry fee, and the entertainment proved so popular that within a year it was necessary to find a larger home. An annual rent of £5 was agreed to move in 1877 to a rented field in Muntz Street.

It was there that the seeds of the fierce rivalry between Birmingham and Aston Villa were sown. The two clubs faced each other for the first time in September 1879. Small Heath won "by a goal and a disputed goal to nil", and afterwards Villa's players – as well as some of the home ones – complained about the state of the pitch.

In 1890 they began playing competitive football in the Football Alliance, and after finishing third in only their second season they were voted into the Football League. Almost inevitably their first match was against Aston Villa, with 20,000 people in attendance to see them beaten 2-1.

The club was growing in wealth, and set a precedent in 1888 by becoming the first football club to register as a limited company. They were run by a committee which also picked the team, but it was decided a different approach was needed and Alf Jones was appointed in the summer of 1892 as the club's first secretary-manager. Under his guidance, Small Heath became the first League club to score 100 goals in a season (there were just 28 matches played at that time).

As the 19th century drew to a close, football was gradually taking over from cricket as England's most popular national game and the players were becoming celebrities. After two brief seasons in the top division of the Football League, Small Heath had been relegated back to the second tier. Nevertheless, goalscorers such as Frank Mobley and Walter Abbott, who still holds the club record of 42 goals in a season, were local heroes who did much to sow the seeds for the future of the club.

Record in the 19th Century

Aston Villa:

Season	League	P	W	D	L	F	A	Pts	Position
1888–89	Div 1	22	12	5	5	61	43	29	2
1889–90	Div 1	22	7	5	10	43	51	19	8
1890–91	Div 1	22	7	4	11	45	58	18	9
1891–92	Div 1	26	15	0	11	89	56	30	4
1892–93	Div 1	30	16	3	11	73	62	35	4
1893–94	Div 1	30	19	6	5	84	42	44	1
1894–95	Div 1	30	17	5	8	82	43	39	3
1895–96	Div 1	30	20	5	5	78	45	45	1
1896–97	Div 1	30	21	5	4	73	38	47	1
1897–98	Div 1	30	14	5	11	61	51	33	6
1898–99	Div 1	34	19	7	8	76	40	45	1
1899–1900	Div 1	34	22	6	6	77	35	50	1

FA Cup

1879–80	Withdrew after reaching third round
1880–81	2-3 v Stafford Road Works (fourth round)
1881–82	2-4 v Wednesbury Old Athletic (fourth round)

1882–83   3-4 v Notts County (fifth round)

1883–84   1-6 v Queen's Park (Glasgow) (fifth round)

1884–85   0-0, 0-3 v West Bromwich Albion (third round)

1885–86   0-2 v Derby County (second round)

1886–87   2-0 v West Bromwich Albion (final at Kennington Oval)

1887–88   1-3 v Preston North End (fifth round)

1888–89   1-8 v Blackburn Rovers (third round)

1889–90   1-4 v Notts County (second round)

1890–91   0-3 v Stoke (second round)

1891–92   0-3 v West Bromwich Albion (final at Kennington Oval)

1892–93   4-5 v Darwen (first round)

1893–94   2-3 v Sheffield Wednesday (third round)

1894–95   1-0 v West Bromwich Albion (final at Crystal Palace)

1895–96   2-4 v Derby County (first round)

1896–97   3-2 v Everton (final at Crystal Palace)

1897–98   0-1 v Derby County (first round)

1898–99   1-2 v Nottingham Forest (first round)

1899–1900 1-1, 0-0, 1-2 v Millwall (third round)

Birmingham:

Season	League	P	W	D	L	F	A	Pts	Position
1889–90	FA	22	6	5	11	44	67	17	10
1890–91	FA	22	7	2	13	58	66	16	10
1891–92	FA	22	12	5	5	53	36	29	3
1892–93	FA	22	17	2	3	90	35	36	1
1893–94	Div 2	28	21	0	7	103	44	42	2
1894–95	Div 1	30	9	7	14	50	74	25	12
1895–96	Div 1	30	8	4	18	39	79	20	15
1896–97	Div 2	30	16	5	9	69	47	37	4
1897–98	Div 2	30	16	4	10	58	50	36	6
1898–99	Div 2	34	17	7	10	85	50	41	8
1899–1900	Div 2	34	20	6	8	78	38	46	3

FA = Football Alliance

FA Cup

1881–82	0-6 v Wednesbury Old Athletic (second round)
1882–83	3-3, 2-6 v Stafford Road Works (second round)
1883–84	1-1, 2-3 v Birmingham Excelsior (first round)
1884–85	0-2 v Birmingham Excelsior (first round)
1885–86	0-4 v West Bromwich Albion (semi-final)
1886–87	1-3 v Mitchell's St George (first round)
1887–88	0-4 v Aston Villa (second round)
1888–89	2-3 v West Bromwich Albion (first round)
1889–90	1-2 v Wolverhampton Wanderers (second round)
1890–91	Disqualified for fielding unregistered player in qualifying rounds
1891–92	0-2 v Sheffield Wednesday (second round)
1892–93	0-2 v Burnley (first round)
1893–94	3-4 v Bolton (first round)
1894–95	1-2 v West Bromwich Albion (first round)
1895–96	1-4 v Bury (first round)
1896–97	1-2 v Notts County (first round)
1897–98	1-2 v Burslem Port Vale (qualifying round)
1898–99	2-2, 1-2 v Stoke (second round)
1899–1900	0-0, 0-2 v Walsall (second round)

Birmingham were formed as Small Heath Alliance, before changing their name in 1905 to Birmingham, and then adding the word City in 1945. For simplicity they will be referred to as just "Birmingham" in statistical sections.

5th November 1887

FA Cup – Third Round

Small Heath Alliance 0

Aston Villa 4

Green (2), Albert A. Brown, Allen

Attendance 12,000

SMALL HEATH: *Charsley, Evetts, Barlow, Farley, Simms, Morris, W. Dixon, Adams, Smith, A. Stanley, Figures*

ASTON VILLA: *Warner, Coulton, Cox, Yates, Devey, Burton, Albert A. Brown, Green, Hunter, Allen, Hodgetts*

The draw for the second round of the FA Cup could not have created more excitement. Aston Villa were the proud holders, having beaten West Bromwich Albion at Kennington Oval seven months earlier.

That was a performance which had stoked-up the emerging rivalry between Birmingham's two biggest clubs. Until then Small Heath had gone furthest in the competition, reaching the semi-final in 1886, but they had been forced to watch Villa lift the trophy and couldn't have had a greater incentive to knock out the holders.

Some 12,000 crammed into the Muntz Street ground – the first five-figure attendance the club had attracted – but it was the visitors who ended up as comfortable winners.

Inside-forward Tommy Green – who would later have the distinction of scoring Villa's first goal in the Football League – was the hero of the hour, finding space to score two goals, but Small Heath had problems coping with the wing play of Albert A. Brown. He had scored 14 goals in the 10 FA Cup games it had taken to reach the final the previous season, and his habit of drifting away from the touchline – unusual in those days – unsettled the home defence and enabled him to increase Villa's lead. Centre-forward Albert Allen got the other goal.

Buoyed by the success against their biggest local rivals, Villa were optimistic about retaining their trophy, but were undone in bizarre fashion when they met Preston North End in the fifth round. The crowd was so big that spectators constantly came onto the pitch, and with Villa leading 1-0 it was agreed by the captains that the game should not be played out as a Cup tie but completed as a friendly. However, after Preston had won 3-1 they claimed the tie, and on appeal the FA sided with them.

1ˢᵗ September 1894

Division One

Aston Villa 2

Smith, Gordon

Small Heath 1

Hands

Attendance: **20,000**

ASTON VILLA: *Wilkes, Baird, Welford, Reynolds, Cowan, Russell, Athersmith, Chatt, Gordon, Hodgetts, Smith*

SMALL HEATH: *Partridge, Purves, Oliver, Ollis, Jenkyns, Davey, Hallam, Walton, Mobley, Wheldon, Hands*

Six seasons after their committee man William McGregor had conceived the idea of the Football League, Aston Villa were the new champions. Inspired by their centre-forward John Devey's 20 goals in a 30-game Division One season, they had taken the title some six points clear of Sunderland and were still basking in that glory as the opening day of the 1894–95 season arrived.

But just as fate had forced them to defend their first FA Cup against their local rivals, so the fixtures decreed that newly promoted Small Heath would be the first team to play at Villa Park.

Some 20,000 spectators were there to see the contest, and having won the title, Villa had signed both a new goalkeeper – Tom Wilkes – and a new centre-forward – Bob Gordon – to strengthen their team.

Left-winger Stephen Smith opened the scoring for Villa, and then Gordon, who had arrived from Heart of Midlothian in Scotland, got a second.

But Birmingham's left-winger Tommy Hands also scored before half-time and the match developed into a tense affair as Villa fought to protect their lead with Wilkes making a couple of important saves.

20th October 1894

Division One
Small Heath 2
Wheldon (pen), Hallam
Aston Villa 2
Gordon, Hodgetts (pen)
Attendance 15,000
SMALL HEATH: *Partridge, Purves, Oliver, Ollis, Jenkyns, Davey, Hallam, Walton, Mobley, Wheldon, Hands*
ASTON VILLA: *Dunning, Spencer, Welford, Burton, Cowan, Russell, Athersmith, Chatt, Gordon, Hodgetts, Woolley*

This was the game that confirmed Small Heath's status as a big club. After clinching promotion from Division Two the previous season, the club's committee had worked feverishly to make improvements to their Muntz Road stadium and now they saw the fruits of their labour. A crowd of 15,000 – the biggest ever to attend a Small Heath home game – packed into all four sides to witness the visit of the champions and passions ran high.

Many League meetings in the years to come would create argument and controversy, and this one set the tone. Fred Wheldon scored for Small Heath from the penalty spot after a disputed decision in the first half, while later in the game Dennis Hodgetts equalized from another contentious spot-kick.

Jack Hallam, whose speed on the right wing had played a large part in the previous season's promotion campaign, got the other goal for the home team who gave what reports at the time described as a "spirited display". Bob Gordon had scored the first goal for Villa.

It was to be one of the last things he did for the club, however. His arrival from Scotland was intended to improve Villa's team but instead the committee chose to restore John Devey to the centre-forward position and Gordon was sold to Leicester Fosse having played just four games and scored two goals – both of them against Small Heath!

7ᵗʰ September 1895

Division One

Aston Villa 7

Campbell 4, Devey 2, Cowan

Small Heath 3

Walton, Mobley, Hands

Attendance: 14,000

ASTON VILLA: *Wilkes, Spencer, Welford, Reynolds, Cowan, Crabtree, Athersmith, Devey, Campbell, Hodgetts, Smith*

SMALL HEATH: *Roach, Purves, Oliver, Ollis, Jolley, Devey, Hallam, Walton, Mobley, Wheldon, Hands*

Villa's last attempt to sign a centre-forward from Scotland had not worked out, but with the influence of William McGregor, the club were not afraid to return north of the border as they tried to improve their team and regain the First Division title.

They persuaded a 24-year-old player from Celtic, Johnny Campbell, to move south in the summer of 1895 and he made a fairly quiet debut in a 1-0 win over West Bromwich Albion. A week later, though, he exploded into action scoring four goals that left Small Heath stunned as Villa raced into a 5-0 lead by half-time. Campbell, a Scottish international, simply had too much strength and ability for the opposing defenders to deal with and he fitted so quickly into Villa's forward line that goals flowed.

John Devey and James Cowan got the other two – and although Small Heath could take some comfort in fighting back to "win the second half", it was already Campbell's day. The result gave Villa – and their new centre-forward – the impetus they needed and they went on to finish top of the League, with Campbell scoring 26 goals.

26th October 1895

Division One

Small Heath 1

Jones

Aston Villa 4

Devey 2, Reynolds, Campbell

Attendance: 10,000

SMALL HEATH: *Meates, Purves, Oliver, Ollis, Haynes, Jolley, Hallam, Jones, Mobley, Wheldon, Hands*

ASTON VILLA: *Wilkes, Spencer, Elliott, Reynolds, Cowan, Crabtree, Athersmith, Devey, Campbell, Hodgetts, Smith*

If the 7-3 romp at their Perry Barr ground had set Aston Villa up for the season, then it was having the opposite effect on their neighbours.

By the time some 10,000 were at Muntz Street to see the return fixture, secretary-manager Alfred Jones had seen his team win only one game and suffer seven defeats. He had already changed goalkeeper twice, and the next experiment was to bring in a young lad from Eastbourne called Bill Meates. At half-time it was beginning to look a promising decision with the scores level and Aston Villa's attack, which had followed up on their early promise by hitting four against both Derby and Everton, was struggling to find a way through.

However, things changed and with winger Charlie Athersmith becoming influential, the goals began to flow. John Devey, switched to inside-forward to make room for Johnny Campbell's arrival, scored twice while Campbell himself got another and wing-half Jack "Baldy" Reynolds also scored – one of 17 goals in his 96 appearances in a Villa shirt. Small Heath at least salvaged some pride when Bill Jones scored, but it was little consolation in a season where defending would continue to be a problem. It ended with them relegated, having let in 79 goals in 30 League games.

Chapter Two

The Early 20th Century

If Aston Villa had been the ground-breaking side of the Victorian era, then as the 20th century began it was Birmingham's turn to innovate. Having already set an example to others by becoming a limited company and then appointing a team manager, they were determined not to be overshadowed by their more successful neighbours.

As most of the clubs emerged in the late 19th century there was a clear division between the directors and committee men who ran them, and the players. English sport still had a class division between amateurs and professionals. But Small Heath's committee broke that down by inviting former player Harry Morris to join their board.

His youthful enthusiasm and ambition drove the club forward at a time when their ground in Muntz Street was becoming too outdated to cope with the demands of the Football League. He oversaw the renovation of the stadium, but knew that what was really needed was a new home altogether – and he was the man who looked at a "wilderness of stagnant water and muddy slopes" to envisage the potential of how 7.5 acres of waste ground could be transformed from the disused home of a brickworks company into St Andrew's.

The Blues moved in on Boxing Day of 1906, but by then another significant change had taken place. At a dinner given to the players, director Mr R.D. Todd proposed that "as we are the only League club in Birmingham, it would be opportune to change the club's name to Birmingham City". It was pointed out that Aston Villa's home, in the borough of Aston Manor, was outside of the city boundaries. The move was adopted – although curiously with an amendment that the word City would not be included at that time.

Aston Villa's era of dominance in the First Division had ended at the turn of the century, and although they were runners-up in 1903 and won the FA Cup two years later, they found they could no longer be guaranteed of trophies as other clubs grew stronger. In 1906 they finished below Birmingham in the League table for the first time and responded by signing new players. By 1910 they were champions again, ending the season five points clear of Liverpool. Runners-up the following season, they finished second again in 1913 and 1914 before the onset of the First World War caused football to be suspended.

Record before the First World War

Aston Villa:

Season	League	P	W	D	L	F	A	Pts	Position
1900–01	Div 1	34	10	10	14	45	51	30	15
1901–02	Div 1	34	13	8	13	42	40	34	8
1902–03	Div 1	34	19	3	12	61	40	41	2
1903–04	Div 1	34	17	7	10	70	48	41	5
1904–05	Div 1	34	19	4	11	63	43	42	4
1905–06	Div 1	38	17	6	15	72	56	40	8
1906–07	Div 1	38	19	6	13	78	52	44	5
1907–08	Div 1	38	17	9	12	77	59	43	2
1908–09	Div 1	38	14	10	14	58	56	38	7
1909–10	Div 1	38	23	7	8	84	42	53	1
1910–11	Div 1	38	22	7	9	69	41	51	2
1911–12	Div 1	38	17	7	14	76	63	41	6
1912–13	Div 1	38	19	12	7	86	52	50	2

| 1913–14 | Div 1 | 38 | 19 | 6 | 13 | 65 | 50 | 44 | 2 |
| 1914–15 | Div 1 | 38 | 13 | 11 | 14 | 62 | 72 | 37 | 14 |

FA Cup

1900–01	2-2, 0-3 v Sheffield United (semi-final)
1901–02	2-2, 1-2 v Stoke (first round)
1902–03	0-3 v Bury (semi-final)
1903–04	0-1 v Tottenham Hotspur (second round)
1904–05	2-0 v Newcastle United (final at Crystal Palace)
1905–06	1-5 v Manchester United (third round)
1906–07	0-2 v Bolton Wanderers (second round)
1907–08	0-2 v Manchester United (third round)
1908–09	0-2 v Nottingham Forest (first round)
1909–10	1-2 v Manchester City (third round)
1910–11	1-2 v Manchester United (second round)
1911–12	1-1, 0-1 v Reading (second round)
1912–13	1-0 v Sunderland (final at Crystal Palace)
1913–14	0-2 v Liverpool (semi-final)
1914–15	0-1 v Manchester City (second round)

Birmingham:

Season	League	P	W	D	L	F	A	Pts	Position
1900–01	Div 2	34	19	10	5	57	24	48	2
1901–02	Div 1	34	11	8	15	47	45	30	17
1902–03	Div 2	34	24	3	7	74	36	51	2
1903–04	Div 1	34	11	8	15	39	52	30	11
1904–05	Div 1	34	17	5	12	54	38	39	7
1905–06	Div 1	38	17	7	14	65	59	41	7
1906–07	Div 1	38	15	8	15	52	52	38	9
1907–08	Div 1	38	9	12	17	40	60	30	20
1908–09	Div 2	38	14	9	15	58	61	37	11
1909–10	Div 2	38	8	7	23	42	78	23	20
1910–11	Div 2	38	12	8	18	42	64	32	16

1911–12	Div 2	38	14	6	18	55	59	34	12
1912–13	Div 2	38	18	10	10	59	44	46	3
1913–14	Div 2	38	12	10	16	48	60	34	14
1914–15	Div 2	38	17	9	12	62	39	43	6

FA Cup

1900–01	0-0, 0-1 v Aston Villa (third round)
1901–02	1-2 v Portsmouth (first round)
1902–03	1-2 v Derby County (first round)
1903–04	1-1, 1-3 v Manchester United (second round)
1904–05	0-2 v Portsmouth (first round)
1905–06	2-2, 0-3 v Newcastle United (fourth round)
1906–07	1-2 v Liverpool (first round)
1907–08	1-1, 1-2 v West Bromwich Albion (first round)
1908–09	2-5 v Portsmouth (first round)
1909–10	1-4 v Leicester Fosse (first round)
1910–11	1-1, 0-2 v Oldham Athletic (first round)
1911–12	0-0, 0-3 v Barnsley (first round)
1912–13	0-4 v Manchester City (first round)
1913–14	1-2 v Queens Park Rangers (second round)
1914–15	2-3 v Oldham Athletic (third round)

23rd March 1901

FA Cup – Third Round

Small Heath 0

Aston Villa 0

Attendance: 18,000

SMALL HEATH: *Robinson, Archer, Pratt, Adey, Wigmore, Leake, Bennett, Aston, McMillan, Main, Wharton*

ASTON VILLA: *George, Crabtree, Evans, Bowman, Cowan, Wilkes, Lloyd, Athersmith, Devey, Garraty, Templeton*

Six years after they had last met, the wonders of the FA Cup draw paired the two great rivals once more.

As a new century began, Villa were at the peak of their powers as a club. They had moved from their original Perry Barr home to their new Aston Lower Grounds stadium and gone from strength to strength, winning the League and FA Cup Double in 1897, and then successive First Division titles in 1899 and 1900.

Things were looking up at Small Heath, too. Bob McRoberts was emerging as a prolific centre-forward and a couple of weeks before this third-round tie he had scored five goals in a 10-1 thrashing of Blackpool. The FA Cup had been disrupted because the first round was postponed following the death of Queen Victoria, but that only added to the sense of anticipation as a crowd of 18,000 — a record attendance at Muntz Street — squeezed in to wait for the action.

In the event it was a let-down, a goalless draw in which both defences dominated and much depended on the excellent defending of Villa's Jimmy Crabtree. He had been overlooked by the England selectors and his performance led to suggestions that there was bias at the FA in favour of those who played for certain clubs. Match reports say that "Crabtree and Evans played a grand game, as did Wilkes". Small Heath certainly had the better of the match and were unfortunate to be taken to a replay.

27th March 1901

FA Cup – Third Round Replay

Aston Villa 1

Garraty

Small Heath 0

Attendance: 15,000

SMALL HEATH: *Robinson, Archer, Pratt, Walton, Wigmore, Leake, Bennett, Aston, McMillan, Main, Wharton*

ASTON VILLA: *George, Crabtree, Evans, Bowman, Cowan, Wilkes, Templeton, Athersmith, Devey, Garraty, Smith*

Horrendous weather accompanied the replay. Heavy snowstorms swirled around the Birmingham area all day, and great efforts were made to get the pitch in a condition for play to go ahead. The cold drove away spectators – a few days after 18,000 had crammed into Muntz Street, only 15,000 made it for the replay – although there were complaints about high prices for admission which also affected the attendance.

The weather didn't get any better. At one point the game had to be held up for four minutes because the snow was so intense that the referee couldn't see what was going on.

In the conditions it was tough for either team to make much headway, and another tense match ensued in which two teams who had been scoring goals freely found it difficult to break through.

It was still goalless as the final whistle blew, meaning extra-time had to be played during which Billy Garraty, who was establishing a reputation as a supremely fit forward, had the energy to find the goal which broke the deadlock.

It was one of only six defeats in the entire campaign for Small Heath, who ended the season as runners-up behind Grimsby in Division Two, and the stage was set for rivalries to resume in the Football League. The match report of the time said: "The long and the short of it is that Small Heath are practically as good a side as the Villa. Above all I congratulate Alec Leake, who is a great half back and a good general."

12th October 1901

Division One
Small Heath 0
Aston Villa 2
Devey, Bache
Attendance: 23,000
SMALL HEATH: *Robinson, Goldie, Archer, Walton, Wigmore, Leake, Athersmith, Aston, McRoberts, McMillan, Wharton*

ASTON VILLA: *George, Noon, Crabtree, Wilkes, Wood, Harris, Clarke, Devey, Garraty, Bache, Templeton*

Villa's season had started badly, and by the time they came to resume hostilities against their traditional rivals as the early autumn sun began to cast shadows over Muntz Street, there were clear signs that their dominant position in English football was beginning to wane.

They had won only once in their first seven fixtures, and more worryingly, a side which had once scored goals freely was finding it hard to break down defences, with only five goals scored until then.

The committee chose to bring back former captain John Devey, who according to reports at the time had been considered to be "on the shelf", to solve the problem and had just paid £400 to Bury to sign young Scottish striker James "Jasper" McLuckie.

Small Heath, having won promotion, were actually above Villa in the table at this point and full of optimism about the season ahead. Inside-forward Jack Aston, signed from Woolwich Arsenal, had built up a strong understanding with fellow forwards Bob McRoberts and Johnny McMillan and they had shared nine goals in the previous five matches.

The anticipation of a possible first competitive victory over their rivals brought a huge crowd, and the gates were closed before kick-off. There followed a rush of people from outside trying to get in, and gatekeepers barred their way with chunks of wood.

In that atmosphere it was a tense first half, and Small Heath had a number of chances to take the lead as they dominated the play.

But eventually John Devey took a chance to make a breakthrough for the visitors, and then Stourbridge-born Joe Bache got another goal to make the win safe.

26ᵗʰ December 1901

Division One

Aston Villa 1

McLuckie

Small Heath 0

Attendance: 50,000

ASTON VILLA: *George, Shutt, Crabtree, Perry, Wood, Wilkes, Clarke, Garraty, McLuckie, Bache, Marriott*

SMALL HEATH: *Robinson, Goldie, Bunch, Adey, Wigmore, Leake, Athersmith, Leonard, McRoberts, McMillan, Wharton*

Villa's strong Scottish influence came to the fore again with the signing of Jasper McLuckie.

Aged 22 and born in Glasgow, he had played in Bury's side in the 1900 FA Cup final and was seen as the player to perk up a front line that had lost its way. He was one of three players signed in the same week – the others being winger Bill Marriott and former West Bromwich Albion wing-half Tom Perry.

They came just too late to play in the first derby match.

But shaking up the team had the desired effect, with McLuckie scoring 10 goals in his first seven games, and the thought of a Boxing Day encounter with Small Heath encouraged another huge crowd, with 50,000 inside Villa Park by kick-off time. Thankfully the bigger ground was better equipped to deal with the numbers and there was no repeat of the scenes that had accompanied the match at Muntz Street.

On the field Small Heath's own fortunes had begun to wane, and they were caught out early in the game when McLuckie seized a chance to give Villa the lead.

From there the visitors put up a spirited display, though, and it needed Villa's goalkeeper Billy George to turn in one of the best performances of his 360 games for the club to make sure of the victory.

By the time the two teams met again, in a friendly in April 1902 to raise funds to help victims of the Ibrox Stadium disaster, Small Heath had slid to second from bottom and were relegated alongside Manchester City.

19th September 1903

Division One

Small Heath 2

Wilcox, Robertson

Aston Villa 2

Garraty, Pearson (pen)

Attendance: 25,000

SMALL HEATH: Robinson, Goldie, Wassell, Dougherty, Wigmore, Howard, Athersmith, Robertson, McRoberts, Wilcox, Leonard

ASTON VILLA: George, Spencer, Noon, Pearson, Wood, Wilkes, Brawn, Garraty, McLuckie, Bache, Niblo

Small Heath returned to the First Division at the first attempt, finishing runners-up to Manchester City, and that produced great enthusiasm as their rivalry with Villa was renewed. Off the field, the club were taking steps forward, having invited former player Harry Morris to join the board of directors to provide assistance and advice on the selection of new players.

This was another match which added to the tradition of controversy, however. Villa took the lead after just eight minutes when Tommy Niblo whipped the ball into the front of goal and Billy Garraty got on the end of it to head home.

Niblo, a clever winger, then deceived Small Heath defender Jim Dougherty into tripping him inside the penalty area. Niblo, however, according to the reports had been offside when he received the ball, but "Mr Kinscott the referee was some way behind the play and did not grasp the fact."

Any argument came to nothing, and wing-half Joe Pearson

"scored with the greatest ease".

After half-time Small Heath, galvanized by their sense of injustice, fought their way back into the game. Niblo spoiled his other good play by being offside continually, and the chain of free-kicks helped Small Heath encourage some dominance.

Fred Wilcox missed an excellent chance, but atoned for that error by scoring with a header and within a minute Small Heath were level, Jim Robertson finding the net.

Small Heath scented their chance for victory, and it needed an outstanding save by Billy George to prevent them from scoring a winner.

16th January 1904

Division One
Aston Villa 1
Brawn
Small Heath 1
Green
Attendance: 20,000
ASTON VILLA: *George, Spencer, Leake, Pearson, Wood, Wilkes, Brawn, Hall, Niblo, Bache, Lockett*
SMALL HEATH: *Robinson, Glover, Stokes, Goldie, Chaplin, Howard, Athersmith, Green, Jones, Leonard, Field*

Small Heath's team had begun to recover after a dreadful first half to the season, beginning the new year with a draw at Sheffield United and then beating Newcastle 3-0.

But two FA Cup replays against Manchester United had left a heavy toll of injuries, and with experienced centre-half Walter Wigmore suspended it was a weakened side which travelled to Villa Park.

New signing Jack Glover, a former West Brom defender who had moved back to the Midlands after playing for Liverpool, was appointed as Small Heath's captain for the first time and made his debut although he was "not yet in best condition". Despite those concerns over his fitness, he "performed fairly well at right back for his new club".

Snow was falling as the crowd filed into the ground, but the pitch was in playable condition, and Small Heath had the better of the early exchanges.

But after 20 minutes right-winger Billy Brawn put Villa in front, hitting "a beauty, a long fast daisy cutter that would have beaten any custodian".

From there Villa got on top without ever being able to find a second goal, and with five minutes left they were made to pay when Small Heath applied increasing pressure and Benny Green headed the equalizer.

29th October 1904

Division One
Aston Villa 2
Brawn (pen), Garraty
Small Heath 1
Wilcox
Attendance: 50,000
ASTON VILLA: *George, Miles, Evans, Pearson, Leake, Windmill, Brawn, Garraty, Matthews, Bache, Lochett*
SMALL HEATH: *Robinson, Glover, Stokes, Beer, Wigmore, Dougherty, McRoberts, Green, Jones, Wilcox, Field*

Played on a beautiful autumn afternoon, the football was as bad-tempered as the weather was sunny. Reports say there were frequent fouls, "and at one point Mr Kinscott the referee had to interfere to prevent Green and Windmill from coming to blows."

In fact even the referee himself was hurt during one mêlée, and had to surrender the whistle to Mr Tunnicliffe for a brief time to allow him to recover.

Fred Wilcox, an inside-right recruited from Bristol Rovers the previous season, showed more calm than most when centre-forward Billy Jones found an opening for him and he scored from close range.

Villa made great attempts to equalize, but wasted their opportunities through wretched shooting, with Garraty in particular firing straight at Small Heath keeper Robinson.

But a foul by Bob McRoberts undid all the good defensive work. He tripped Joe Bache, and Mr Kinscott, by this time back in charge of the whistle, awarded the penalty kick from which Billy Brawn equalized.

There was more controversy to come. Small Heath conceded another free-kick on the edge of their area which Villa centre-half Alex Leake, considered a bit of a "traitor" as he was born in Small Heath, flighted into the area. Robinson came to collect the ball only to be bundled into his own goal by Garraty, but the referee ruled it was a fair charge and allowed the goal to stand.

25th February 1905

Division One
Small Heath 0
Aston Villa 3
Pearson, Hampton, Windmill
Attendance: **32,000**
SMALL HEATH: *Robinson, Glover, Stokes, Beer, Wigmore, Dougherty, Tickle, Green, Jones, Wilcox, Field*
ASTON VILLA: *George, Spencer, Miles, Pearson, Wilkes, Windmill, Brawn, Garraty, Hampton, Bache, Hall*

After the unpleasantness of the derby earlier in the season, there was much focus on this match and discussion beforehand on the importance of fine behaviour.

The Blues had carried out a good deal of work to improve their

Muntz Street stadium, although the club was already beginning to realize that it was not going to be the right venue for a permanent home. The landlord, Mr Gessey, had turned down approaches to buy the freehold, and had also refused permission for any major extensions to be made.

The gates were closed on a 30,000 attendance, but it was estimated that another 2,000 spectators found their way in by either climbing gates or walls.

Small Heath had won four of their previous five matches, including a 4-1 success at home to Wolves, and again enthusiasm was running high.

But despite early pressure they conceded a goal scored by Villa's right-half Joe Pearson, and never found a way back into the game.

Harry Hampton, who had been signed by Villa from Wellington the previous summer, was beginning to establish himself as a feared and physical centre-forward, and he made it two.

Once left-half Jack Windmill scored Villa's third, the game was all over as a contest.

The season was to end well for both clubs. Villa went on to win the FA Cup, while Small Heath got back to winning ways by scoring four at Blackburn the following weekend and ultimately finished seventh in the First Division table.

16th September 1905

Division One
Birmingham 2
Jones, Mounteney
Aston Villa 0
Attendance: 34,000
BIRMINGHAM: *Robinson, Glover, Stokes, Beer, Wigmore, Dougherty, Green, Mounteney, Jones, Wilcox, Field*
ASTON VILLA: *George, Noon, Miles, Pearson, Leake, Windmill, Brawn, Garraty, Hampton, Bache, Hall*

A new era began for the Blues in the best possible way. Earlier in 1905 it had been proposed and passed that Small Heath should change the club's name. Director Mr R.D. Todd pushed forward the plan, pointing out that as Aston Villa played "outside the city of Birmingham in the borough of Aston Manor", it would be opportune to establish the identity as the only League club in England's second city.

There was opposition to the move. The *Daily Mirror*'s report of this match mentions "Birmingham – how strange this name sounds". Other newspapers referred to the team as "the Small Heath club now masquerading as Birmingham".

Perhaps it was the change of name that had the desired effect – who can say – but this was the game when Aston Villa were finally made to taste defeat against their local rivals.

Both teams were unbeaten in their first couple of fixtures, and again the Muntz Street gates had to be closed with the ground filled to capacity.

The official attendance remains recorded at the maximum 30,000, but it was believed that another 4,000 broke through the gates and there were spectators sitting around the edge of the ground and close to the touchlines.

Birmingham played with "a combination of grit and go" which seemed to leave Aston Villa's players second best all over the pitch.

Harry Hampton, who had scored a hat-trick in a 5-0 win over Liverpool a few days earlier, was given no quarter by Birmingham's defence in which centre-half Walter Wigmore set the example of committed play.

Wild celebrations were sparked as Tommy Jones and Arthur Mounteney, a summer recruit from Leicester Fosse, scored the historic goals.

20th January 1906

Division One

Aston Villa 1

Bache

Birmingham 3

Mounteney, Jones, Dougherty

Attendance: 40,000

ASTON VILLA: *Cooch, Noon, Evans, Pearson, Leake, Wilkes, Brawn, Garraty, Hampton, Bache, Hall*

BIRMINGHAM: *Robinson, Glover, Hartwell, Cornan, Wigmore, Dougherty, Harper, Green, Jones, Mounteney, Anderson*

They say form goes out of the window in derby matches, and that was never truer than in this encounter.

Having beaten Villa for the first time in their history, Birmingham arrived at Villa Park in the middle of a mid-season slump. They had celebrated Boxing Day by thrashing Middlesbrough 7-0, with centre-forward Benny Green making history by becoming the club's first player to score five goals in one match.

But that was followed by four defeats in a row and optimism wasn't high as they set off to play their traditional rivals.

What followed was another game to add to the bitterness which has always surrounded this rivalry. Villa full-back Albert Evans suffered a broken leg in a tackle early in the game, in what the *Daily Mirror*'s reporter described as "a deplorable accident". It was an injury which was to end the Villa career of a player who had been part of the side which won the Double nine years earlier, and it started a series of unsavoury challenges.

As the *Mirror*'s report said: "It is regrettable to hear that some of the players allowed their tempers to run riot, for the game is not improved thereby."

Down to 10 men in the days long before substitutes were allowed, Villa managed to score a goal through Joe Bache.

But with a team which was already weakened by missing several key players through injury, most notably their other first-choice full-back Howard Spencer, Villa couldn't cope and Birmingham could have scored more than the three from Arthur Mounteney, Billy Jones and Jim Dougherty.

It was a significant result for Birmingham. After beating Villa in a League match for the first time they had done the double – and they went on to finish seventh in the First Division with 41 points, a point and a place above their bitter rivals.

15th September 1906

Division One
Aston Villa 4
Greenhalgh, Hall, Walters, Hampton (pen)
Birmingham 1
Mounteney
Attendance: 40,000
ASTON VILLA: *George, Spencer, Miles, Greenhalgh, Boden, Codling, Hall, Garraty, Hampton, Bache, Walters*
BIRMINGHAM: *Robinson, Glover, Stokes, Beer, Wigmore, Dougherty, Harper, Green, Jones, Mounteney, Anderson*

Villa's response to being beaten twice by their neighbours in the previous season had been to shake things up, most notably by signing centre-half Sam Greenhalgh from Bolton.

The 24-year-old had impressed in the Bolton side which reached the 1904 FA Cup final, and as Villa feared their defending was not up to scratch they took steps to improve things.

By the time Birmingham came to Villa Park in mid-September, the revamped team was sitting at the top of the early First Division table with three wins and a defeat to their name.

Meanwhile, Birmingham had suffered a disappointing opening to the season, with just one draw and two defeats from three games.

Villa captain Howard Spencer had seen how his club's pride was stung by the two defeats the previous season, and was at his imperious best in defence as his team "utterly routed their neighbours", according to the *Daily Mirror* report.

Greenhalgh was hailed as the best player on the field – and it was a smart piece of work on his part which led to him scoring the first goal and the only one of the first half.

Villa continued to be the cleverer side all the way through the game, as Albert Hall and Joe Walters helped themselves to goals after the interval before Harry Hampton completed the scoring with a late penalty.

Birmingham had little to offer other than a consolation goal scored by Arthur Mounteney.

Villa were top of the table that evening – while Birmingham were rooted to the bottom.

19th January 1907

Division One

Birmingham 3

Glover, Mounteney, Green (pen)

Aston Villa 2

Chapple, Walters

Attendance: **60,000**

BIRMINGHAM: *Robinson, Glover, Stokes, Beer, Wigmore, Cornan, Harper, Green, Jones, Mounteney, Anderson*

ASTON VILLA: *George, Corbett, Miles, Greenhalgh, Buckley, Codling, Walters, Cantrel, Hampton, Chapple, Evans*

It hadn't only been the two victories over Aston Villa in the previous season, or the seventh-place finish that convinced Birmingham they were a club on the move.

In the winter of 1904 director Harry Morris had visited the disused site of a former brickworks company. Covering some 7.5

acres it was derelict, but Morris, a former Birmingham player, looked beyond the rubble strewn across waste ground – he described it as "a wilderness of stagnant water and muddy slopes" – and could envisage the site as a much-needed new stadium for his beloved football club.

Birmingham had moved fast, secured the land on a 21-year lease, and by February of 1906 work began on building St Andrew's. The new stadium, complete with a giant embankment of 110 steps that could accommodate 48,000 people, opened for business on Boxing Day – but it was on 19th January that it could be seen in its full glory.

The *Daily Mirror* account of the time relates that "over 40,000 people were at Birmingham to see Birmingham beat Aston Villa by 3 to 2". Official figures held by the club put the attendance at some 60,000.

Villa were in no mood to let their hosts enjoy a party day, however, and went into the lead by half-time with Fred Chapple and Joe Walters on the scoresheet while full-back Jack Glover scored for Birmingham.

But, urged on by the giant crowd, the home team fought back after the break, and almost inevitably Arthur Mounteney, who had scored the last ever goal at Muntz Street, continued his record of success in derby fixtures by getting an equalizer.

Then came the controversy of a penalty award, and Benny Green kept cool to put away the winning goal.

21st September 1907

Division One

Birmingham 2

Eyre, Tickle

Aston Villa 3

Cantrell, Evans, Hall

Attendance: 50,000

BIRMINGHAM: *Robinson, Glover, Stokes, Beer, Wigmore, Dougherty, Tickle, Green, Mounteney, Cornan, Eyre*
ASTON VILLA: *Turner, Miles, Riley, Greenhalgh, J. Logan, Codling, Harper, Cantrell, Hampton, Hall, Evans*

The modern idea of squad rotation was unthinkable at the start of the 20th century. Clubs had a team, and a reserve team, and tended to make changes only when forced to do so by injuries.

So it was a measure of how badly Aston Villa's season had begun that after losing their first two matches at home to Manchester United and then at Blackburn they had completely reshaped their side.

There were five different players in the line-up at Birmingham compared to the side which had begun the season, including a change of goalkeeper.

Harry Cooch had been dropped after just one game, when he conceded four against United, to allow Billy George, the club's stalwart for the previous eight seasons, to return.

George, aged 33, was suffering from lumbago and after playing two matches was unable to continue, so Villa's committee turned to Horace Turner who had just been signed from Burton Albion.

Turner got through his debut in front of 18,000 at Villa Park without conceding a goal, but the huge crowd at St Andrew's was a nerve-racking experience for him and Birmingham took a half-time lead with a goal by winger Edmund Eyre.

The reports of the day refer to Birmingham's "energetic young team', which was deserving to be in front in a tight game.

But, still smarting from the two defeats the previous season, Villa were determined not to go down a third time and fought their way back.

Jimmy Cantrell and Robert Evans put them in front, and though Charlie Tickle brought the scores back level, in a thrilling finish Albert Hall — switched from his usual position on the wing to play at centre-forward in the absence of Harry Hampton who had gone off injured — grabbed the winner.

18th January 1908

Division One
Aston Villa 2
A. Logan, Hall
Birmingham 3
Eyre, Green (pen), Drake
Attendance: **35,000**
ASTON VILLA: *George, Lyons, Miles, Garraty, J. Logan, Codling, Harper, Hampton, A. Logan, Bache, Hall*
BIRMINGHAM: *Dorrington, W.S. Corbett, Kearns, Beer, Wigmore, Green, Tickle, Bluff, Mounteney, Drake, Eyre*

Edmund Eyre was Birmingham's hero. The winger had been signed at the start of the season from Rotherham, then playing in the Midland League, but had grabbed his chance to show he could perform in the First Division.

While the Blues had been struggling during the first half of the campaign, with only five wins by the time of this derby, Eyre had caught the eye with his pace and trickery on the left flank.

His ability to cut in and score goals had marked him out as a danger man, but Villa were still caught out when after 16 minutes their right-back Tommy Lyons slipped as he tried to deal with a cross from Charlie Tickle, and Eyre pounced on the loose ball to give Billy George no chance.

Villa, who had seen a shot by Benny Green cleared off the line early in the match, were level within a minute as Alec Logan, brother of new captain James, calmly accepted his chance.

But Eyre's trickery continued to cause problems and when he was fouled by Lyons, Green stepped up to convert the penalty.

The foul forced Eyre to go off for treatment, but despite limping heavily he returned to continue the game, and shortly afterwards Tickle's centre presented Alonzo Drake with the chance to make it 3-1 before half-time.

Villa applied pressure after the interval, getting a goal back when Albert Hall pounced onto a loose ball after Jack Dorrington had made a brilliant save.

Dorrington, who had been at the club since 1903 but played barely a handful of games before the 1907–08 season, was hurt trying to prevent the goal, but like Eyre he battled on.

There was more controversy near the end as, with fog swirling around the ground, Villa claimed they should have had a penalty for hand ball, but the decision was not given.

Birmingham thought the win might have been a turning point in their season, and so it proved, but not in the way they hoped. They won only three more matches, finished bottom of the First Division table and were relegated. It would be 14 years before the two Birmingham clubs met in a Football League game again.

Chapter Three

The 1920s

As people strived for a return to normal life after the horrors of the First World War, football became one of the most popular forms of entertainment – and at both Aston Villa and Birmingham they rode the wave of enthusiasm.

Villa especially came back to business with a bang – winning the FA Cup for a record sixth time in 1919–20, the first proper season in peacetime. Inspired by the stout defending of Frank Barson, bought from Barnsley for a club record fee of £2,850, they beat Huddersfield in the final at Stamford Bridge through an extra-time goal by Billy Kirton.

Thanks to the goalscoring exploits of new heroes Billy Walker and Len Capewell, they reached another final four years later – this time at Wembley Stadium which had memorably hosted the "White Horse Final" a year earlier. The game ended in disappointment with a 2-0 defeat to Newcastle, but Walker and Capewell continued to form a successful forward partnership in the following seasons.

Birmingham, relegated in 1908, had handed responsibility for organizing their team during the war to Frank Richards, who had worked his way up through the club's small office staff after leaving a job in the nearby jewellery quarter. He brought a flair for administration, sometimes leaving the selection and formation of the team to others on the committee, but his ambition helped put together a side that would cement the club's place in the First Division for nearly two decades.

It was Richards who signed centre-forward Joe Bradford, arguably the club's greatest prewar player and definitely their best ever goalscorer. Bradford was just 19 when he signed for the princely sum of £125 from Green Victoria FC in Leicestershire. Born in Peggs Green near Coalville, he had been turned down after trials with both Derby and Aston Villa and was recruited in February 1920 to be the reserve centre-forward.

He didn't score his first goal until a Christmas fixture at West Ham, one of only four appearances in the Second Division Championship-winning campaign of 1920–21, and his first season in the top flight was hardly a roaring success either, with just one goal in 17 appearances.

But by the following year he had made the number 9 shirt his own, and it stayed that way virtually until he left the club in May 1935, having scored an astonishing 267 League and Cup goals in 445 senior appearances.

Richards broke the transfer record to sign Joe Lane, and four months later did it again by paying £3,750 to Ayr for Johnny Crosbie as he looked for players who could feed Bradford's brilliant goalscoring ability.

It would be others who reaped the benefit of his recruitment, however. While Villa continued to run their team by a committee of the directors, Birmingham went through a succession of different managers in the 1920s as they tried to take the club forward. Billy Beer replaced Richards in 1923, and often complained about the attitude of his players during three seasons in charge when the Blues finished 14th, eighth and 14th again. Then another ex-player, Billy Harvey, was given the task, but spent just a year at the helm before moving on to take over Chesterfield. Birmingham's response was to seek an experienced manager, and they turned to Leslie Knighton who had been in charge of Arsenal for six years. His tactical knowledge helped develop a team that would give the Blues their first trip to an FA Cup final.

Record in the 1920s

Aston Villa:

Season	League	P	W	D	L	F	A	Pts	Position
1919–20	Div 1	42	18	6	18	75	73	42	9
1920–21	Div 1	42	18	7	17	63	70	43	10
1921–22	Div 1	42	22	3	17	74	55	47	5
1922–23	Div 1	42	18	10	14	64	51	46	6
1923–24	Div 1	42	18	13	11	52	37	49	6
1924–25	Div 1	42	13	13	16	58	71	39	15
1925–26	Div 1	42	16	12	14	86	76	44	6
1926–27	Div 1	42	18	7	17	81	83	43	10
1927–28	Div 1	42	17	9	16	78	73	43	8
1928–29	Div 1	42	23	4	15	98	81	50	3
1929–30	Div 1	42	21	5	16	92	83	47	4

FA Cup

1919–20	1-0 v Huddersfield Town (final at Stamford Bridge)
1920–21	0-1 v Tottenham Hotspur (fourth round)
1921–22	2-2, 3-4 v Notts County (fourth round)
1922–23	0-1 v Blackburn Rovers (first round)
1923–24	0-2 v Newcastle United (final at Wembley Stadium)
1924–25	1-1, 1-2 v West Bromwich Albion (third round)
1925–26	1-1, 0-2 v Arsenal (fifth round)
1926–27	1-2 v Cardiff City (third round)
1927–28	1-4 v Arsenal (fifth round)
1928–29	0-1 v Portsmouth (semi-final)
1929–30	1-2 v Huddersfield Town (sixth round)

Birmingham:

Season	League	P	W	D	L	F	A	Pts	Position
1919–20	Div 2	42	24	8	10	85	34	56	3
1920–21	Div 2	42	24	10	8	79	38	58	1

1921–22	Div 1	42	15	7	20	48	60	37	18
1922–23	Div 1	42	13	11	18	41	57	37	17
1923–24	Div 1	42	13	13	16	41	49	39	14
1924–25	Div 1	42	17	12	13	49	53	46	8
1925–26	Div 1	42	16	8	18	66	81	40	14
1926–27	Div 1	42	17	4	21	64	73	38	17
1927–28	Div 1	42	13	15	14	70	75	41	11
1928–29	Div 1	42	15	10	17	68	77	40	15
1929–30	Div 1	42	16	9	17	67	62	41	11

FA Cup

1919–20	0-2 v Liverpool (third round)
1920–21	1-2 v Luton (first round)
1921–22	Did not enter
1922–23	1-2 v Huddersfield (first round)
1923–24	0-1 v Huddersfield (first round)
1924–25	1-2 v Liverpool (third round)
1925–26	1-2 v South Shields (fourth round)
1926–27	1-4 v Southampton (fourth round)
1927–28	0-1 v Manchester United (fifth round)
1928–29	0-1 v Chelsea (fourth round)
1929–30	2-2, 0-1 v Arsenal (fourth round)

11th March 1922

Division One

Aston Villa 1

Dickson

Birmingham 1

Liddell

Attendance: 42,000

ASTON VILLA: *Jackson, Jones, Weston, Johnstone, Barson, G. Blackburn, York, Kirton, Dickson, Walker, Dorrell*

BIRMINGHAM: *Tremelling, Roulson, Jones, Liddell, McClure, Barton, Barratt, Crosbie, Bradford, Whitehouse, Foxall*

As the country emerged from the horrors of the First World War, the resumption of League Football was one of the key ways that saw life return to normal.

And after Birmingham won the Second Division title in 1921, the return of competitive matches against their local rivals was eagerly anticipated. It turned into a long wait, however, as the fixture compiler (no computers in those days) settled on a double-header over four days the following March.

Some 42,000 packed Villa Park to see the first encounter. Villa were chasing eventual champions Liverpool at the top of the table, but had just been knocked out of the FA Cup at the hands of Notts County and were keen to make amends.

The Blues, meanwhile, had suffered the indignity of not playing in the FA Cup at all – the club secretary had failed to submit the appropriate form in time! They were also in the middle of a run of just three points from 10 matches and to make matters worse were without captain Frank Womack.

It was typical, however, that form went out of the window as Birmingham started the game well, with Frank Foxall getting in a smart centre and the dangerous Jack Whitehouse narrowly missing with a hard, low shot.

Unfortunately for the Blues, Whitehouse was then injured, and after limping for the rest of the first half he failed to reappear after the interval.

Against 10 men Villa picked up the pace, and goalkeeper Dan Tremelling was forced to save twice from Billy Kirton at close range before Ian Dickson scored in the 47th minute.

That should have been the signal for more home goals, but poor finishing allowed the Blues back in and they created threats through Johnny Crosbie and Joe Bradford before, with 12 minutes left,

George Liddell hit a superb first-time shot for the equalizer. In the time remaining it was Birmingham who did most of the attacking but couldn't find a winner.

15th March 1922

Division One

Birmingham 1

Crosbie

Aston Villa 0

Attendance: 30,000

BIRMINGHAM: *Tremelling, Roulson, Jones, Liddell, McClure, Barton, Barratt, Crosbie, Bradford, Hampton, Foxall*

ASTON VILLA: *Jackson, R. Blackburn, Jones, Johnstone, Barson, G. Blackburn, York, Kirton, Dickson, Walker, Dorrell*

Birmingham's manager Frank Richards had been carefully building his team since taking charge and was establishing a reputation for finding talent.

After guiding the club back to the top flight he had been determined to go on improving the playing resources – during this season Blues used some 31 players as Richards tried to find men who could cope with the demands of First Division football.

But slowly the quality of some of his signings was beginning to emerge.

In the promotion season he had brought in a new centre-forward by the name of Joe Bradford, whom he had spotted playing for Peggs Green Victoria in Leicestershire.

And alongside him was Scottish international inside-forward Johnny Crosbie, persuaded to move south a few months after winning his first international cap while playing for Ayr.

The two of them would go on to be Birmingham stars for the next decade, but at this time they were just beginning to develop an understanding. The promise had been clear during the second half at Villa Park a few days earlier, and they simply carried on where they left off when battle resumed at St Andrew's.

Crosbie gave Blues the lead with a neatly taken goal in the first half, and it was an advantage that the home team managed to protect despite coming under pressure later in the game.

Villa missed several good chances to equalize – so much so that conspiracy theorists set to work with suggestions that they had wanted to help make sure their neighbours remained in the top flight to protect the revenue from the two biggest gates of the season.

The *Birmingham Sports Argus* of the time reported that: "Doubting Thomases have been busy and are quite convinced in their own little minds that Villa were charitably disposed and gave Blues the points to save them from relegation."

17th March 1923

Division One

Birmingham 1

Rawson

Aston Villa 0

Attendance: 50,000

BIRMINGHAM: *Tremelling, Ashurst, Jones, Daws, McClure, Barton, Harvey, Crosbie, Rawson, Bradford, Clark*

ASTON VILLA: *Spiers, Smart, Mort, Moss, Ball, G. Blackburn, York, Roxburgh, Walker, Capewell, Dorrell*

It was a disappointing season for Aston Villa who never showed any consistency – but even so after scoring five away to Huddersfield, with centre-forward Billy Walker getting a hat-trick, they travelled to St Andrew's full of optimism.

But the Blues were in the middle of a good spell of their own. Albert Rawson, signed from Sheffield United, had made a huge impact at centre-forward and had scored in each of his first four League games including a 4-2 win over his former club.

The 23-year-old took just 13 minutes to get on target again, as Edmund Harvey flighted a free-kick so perfectly that he was left with an easy opportunity to head into the far corner.

It stunned Villa, who had been doing well early in the game with Walker showing promise. Rawson should have increased the lead but missed a good chance created by the clever Johnny Crosbie.

Birmingham suffered a blow when wing-half Percy Barton had to go off injured, forcing Joe Bradford to drop into defence for a while – and it got even tougher when Rawson was laid out in a challenge and spent some time off the field before bravely returning, even though he was clearly still suffering the effects.

Captain Alec McClure produced one of the finest of his near-200 displays for the club, marshalling the defence as Villa – with Dicky York always dangerous on the right wing – battled in vain for an equalizer.

24th March 1923

Division One

Aston Villa 3

Capewell, Walker (2 pens)

Birmingham 0

Attendance: 40,000

ASTON VILLA: *Spiers, Smart, Mort, Moss, Ball, G. Blackburn, York, Roxburgh, Walker, Capewell, Dorrell*

BIRMINGHAM: *Tremelling, Ashurst, Jones, Daws, McClure, Barton, Barratt, Crosbie, Rawson, Bradford, Clark*

The rest of the football nation had eyes only on the FA Cup this day – down in London, West Ham and Bolton Wanderers were contesting the first final to be held at Wembley.

Nobody at Villa Park needed a white horse to control the crowd as they did at the Empire Stadium on that famous occasion – but the excitement was no less intense among the 40,000 spectators who came to see if Villa could regain some local pride a week after their defeat at St Andrew's.

They didn't have to wait long to find out. With just five minutes gone Scottish inside-forward John Roxburgh made headway before finding Dicky York who set up Len Capewell for the opening goal.

The Blues missed a good chance to equalize, but Albert Rawson dallied after Johnnie Crosbie set up the chance.

York was again causing problems with his pace and trickery on the right wing, and with 18 minutes gone, a Birmingham defender handled in the penalty area trying to cut out his centre, leaving Billy Walker the chance to firmly plant his shot in the far corner of the net from the penalty spot.

Joe Bradford missed another chance for the Blues just before the interval and it proved costly as with 60 minutes gone Percy Barton and Billy Walker collided after a corner and the referee awarded another penalty.

It was a "wretched decision" according to newspaper reports, which added: "There was nothing whatever to justify it, and the crowd continued to yell 'penalty' whenever the ball was kicked."

Walker showed no mercy, however, as he put away his second spot kick of the game and Birmingham's players drifted out of the game having lost heart.

Villa, a good deal livelier than they had been a week earlier, deserved the win – whatever the argument about the third penalty decision. They were superior in attack, and Birmingham's half-backs found it difficult to control their forwards.

25th August 1923

Division One
Birmingham 3
Bradford (2), Lane
Aston Villa 0
Attendance: 41,305

BIRMINGHAM: *Tremelling, Ashurst, Jones, Dale, McClure, Barton, Harvey, Crosbie, Bradford, Lane, Clark*
ASTON VILLA: *Spiers, Smart, Mort, Moss, Ball, G. Blackburn, York, Kirton, Dickson, Walker, Dorrell*

Joe Bradford was by now maturing into a centre-forward of genuine quality. At the age of 22 he had pace and power, combined with a deadly finish in both feet and had ended the previous season with 18 goals in the League and another in the FA Cup.

He started this campaign the way he meant to go on, scoring a brilliant goal after only two minutes.

Alec McClure broke up a Villa attack and played the ball to Bradford, who with three opponents around him appeared to have no chance but dribbled brilliantly between them and then struck a fierce shot that gave Cyril Spiers no chance.

Birmingham thought they should have had another goal when inside-forward Moses Lane, a courageous character who had won the Military Medal serving in France and Italy during the First World War, was brought down by Frank Moss, but no penalty was given.

But they didn't have to wait much longer, as Lane got his head to a corner taken by Edmund Harvey and directed it beyond the goalkeeper's reach.

Then, straight after half-time, Harvey skipped past three opponents and found Crosbie, whose shot was blocked by Smart but Bradford reacted quickest to tuck away his second and the Blues' third goal.

Birmingham could have had more, with Villa fading in the warmth of the late summer sunshine and only left-winger Arthur Dorrell emerging with any credit.

There was even time for a touch of humour, with a small dog running on to the field to hold up play while police and players scampered around trying to get rid of him.

1st September 1923

Division One
Aston Villa 0
Birmingham 0
Attendance: 59,157
ASTON VILLA: *Spiers, Smart, Jones, Moss, Ball, G. Blackburn, York, Kirton, Walker, Capewell, Dorrell*
BIRMINGHAM: *Tremelling, Womack, Jones, Dale, McClure, Barton, Harvey, Crosbie, Bradford, Lane, Clark*

The opening-day defeat had been hugely damaging for Villa, and even though they recovered to beat Manchester City 2-0 in midweek with goals from Billy Walker and Dicky York, all the focus fell on the following Saturday's return fixture at Villa Park.

But there was a bad start for the home team, as Walker collided with Frank Womack early in the game and needed to be taken off for some time for treatment. He was nursed at the side of the pitch in an attempt to get him back into the game, but eventually had to be carried to the dressing room.

Even with only four forwards, however, Villa were better than they had been at St Andrew's and Birmingham's Alec McClure was having to do a lot to help out his defence.

Villa had clearly learned the lessons of the week before, and had worked out a plan to deal with the threat of Bradford.

The centre-forward had followed his two goals on the opening day with another brace against Liverpool – albeit as part of a 6-2 defeat.

But Villa knew he was the danger man, and had assigned centre-half Tommy Ball to stay man-to-man with him – "a constant bodyguard" as the *Birmingham Sports Argus* described it.

Despite the rivalry continuing to be intense, at least this game was played in a far better spirit without a serious foul in the 90 minutes – and even the injury to Walker was acknowledged as an accident.

But the loss of their centre-forward did weaken Villa. They were the better team in the second half but lacked the forward power to make it count.

11th October 1924

Division One
Birmingham 1
Islip
Aston Villa 0
Attendance: 48,098
BIRMINGHAM: *Tremelling, Womack, Jones, Liddell, Cringan, Barton, W.H. Harvey, Crosbie, Bradford, Islip, Scriven*
ASTON VILLA: *Spiers, Smart, Mort, Moss, Dr V.E. Milne, G. Blackburn, York, Kirton, Capewell, Walker, Dorrell*

Villa's previous season had ended in a Wembley appearance against Newcastle in the FA Cup final – a remarkable achievement given the shock half way through the campaign of the murder of their star centre-half Tommy Ball.

Ball had got into a series of arguments with his landlord about keeping chickens in the back yard. One fateful night the squabble escalated and the landlord, a former policeman, fired a shotgun that left the player fatally wounded.

While attention focused on the subsequent trial – the landlord, George Stagg, was found guilty of murder but reprieved from the death sentence by the new Labour Government – Villa had to deal with the effect on their team.

His place was taken by Dr Vic Milne, a keen amateur sportsman who had also played cricket for Scotland, and who continued to run his practice in Aldridge while turning out in more than 150 First Division matches.

Dr Milne was at centre-half for this game, detailed to take the responsibility for marking Joe Bradford in the same way that Ball had done so successfully a year earlier.

He stood up well to the task – and Villa started the match positively in glorious autumn sunshine with Frank Moss causing danger and Frank Womack excelling in Birmingham's defence.

But once again an injury affected the outcome. Len Capewell collided with a Birmingham defender and had to be carried off, and against 10 men the Blues began to pick up the game.

Cyril Spiers saved well to keep out Bradford, but with half an hour gone Johnny Crosbie began a move that ended with Bradford taking a shot on goal and the ball was deflected into the path of Ernie Islip who scored.

Islip, signed from Huddersfield the previous season, was a key addition to Birmingham's attacking options although he upset the crowd who booed him and Bradford after a couple of rough challenges.

But with Crosbie also adding clever touches the Blues dominated the game.

Capewell returned after the interval and Villa put on pressure without finding a goal – keeper Dan Tremelling producing a stunning double save to keep out Capewell when he seemed certain to score.

14th February 1925

Division One
Aston Villa 1
Capewell
Birmingham 0
Attendance: 60,000
ASTON VILLA: *Jackson, Smart, Bowen, Johnstone, Dr V.E. Milne, Muldoon, York, Kirton, Capewell, Walker, Dorrell*
BIRMINGHAM: *Tremelling, Womack, Jones, Liddell, Cringan, Dale, Harris, Crosbie, Briggs, Islip, Linley*

Ever since the League resumed after the First World War, the fixture list had been designed around "double headers".

With the First Division expanded to 22 clubs, it was considered that the best way to handle fitting the games in was first teams to face each other one week and then meet again at the opposite ground seven days later.

Two games so close together, however, often led to feuds being carried from one week to the next and in this season the practice was ended.

It meant that four months separated the two derby games – as opposed to four days when the clubs had first met after the First World War in 1922. And the effect of the wait following Birmingham's win back in October was to build the anticipation and excitement around the Villa Park contest to massive levels.

The gates were open two hours before kick-off, and some 60,000 were inside the ground when the game began.

Birmingham started best, aided by the skill of Johnny Crosbie, although defender Frank Womack did have to work hard to keep Len Capewell under control.

Villa's football was described as "fast, interesting and clever", but it was the Blues who were the better side for the opening hour and had the first clear-cut chance.

Just after half-time George Briggs set up an opening that Ernie Islip wasn't ready for and so failed to set himself to take.

For long periods Dr Vic Milne was again providing the best medicine for Villa's defence as he again took on the dangerous Joe Bradford.

The home team got lucky when they took the lead after 67 minutes. Full-back Jack Jones made a good tackle on Billy Walker, but the ball broke kindly for Len Capewell who took it on a few feet before driving beyond the reach of Dan Tremelling.

Villa then took the game over but couldn't find a second goal, although Capewell did hit the bar.

17th October 1925

Division One

Aston Villa 3

Walker (2), Capewell

Birmingham 3

Bradford (2), Spiers (og)

Attendance: 52,254

ASTON VILLA: *Spiers, Smart, Mort, Johnstone, Dr V.E. Milne, Moss, York, Kirton, Capewell, Walker, Dorrell*

BIRMINGHAM: *Tremelling, Womack, Jones, Liddell, Cringan, Barton, Harris, Crosbie, Bradford, Briggs, Islip*

We think nothing these days of footballers who play on once they have reached the age of 30 – but back in the 1920s it was a rarity. That makes the feats of Len Capewell at the start of the 1925–26 season all the more remarkable.

Capewell was already a survivor in a far more serious way – he had served with the Royal Engineers in Belgium during the First World War. Returning home he had played non-League football before Villa signed him from Wellington Town when he was already aged 27.

After breaking into the first team and scoring 20 goals in 1923–24 he had faded from the picture in the following season. But in August 1925 he came back with a bang, scoring after just 10 seconds and then four times more in a record opening-day 10-0 rout of Burnley.

By the time the Blues came to Villa Park in October, Capewell was in sensational form with another eight goals in his previous seven matches.

No wonder Villa were in such confident mood, and with just 12 minutes left Billy Walker gave them the lead, dribbling round full-back Jack Jones to tuck the ball away.

The Blues appealed in vain that he had been offside, and kept arguing with Mr J.V. Pennington, the referee, until play kicked off again.

Villa piled on the pressure, and Billy Kirton hit the crossbar before both he and Capewell failed to get to the loose ball in a goalmouth scramble.

But with 40 minutes gone the pressure told. Dicky York made headway on the wing, Frank Womack tried to tackle, but the ball went to Billy Walker whose quick shot on the turn caught Dan Tremelling unawares.

Inevitably it was Capewell who scored Villa's third – another disputed goal with Birmingham claiming for offside. This time Mr Pennington consulted his linesman while the Blues players "swarmed around the referee, appealing far more vigorously than they had even for the first goal".

The protests were to no avail, and it seemed Villa were heading for a comfortable win. Even when with 79 minutes gone Bradford took advantage after a miskick from Tommy Mort, there seemed no danger.

But a minute later goalkeeper Cyril Spiers went for a cross from Wally Harris but dropped the ball at the feet of Bradford, who got his second.

Dr Milne was hurt trying to defend the goal, and had to go to outside left. In his absence Spiers made a save from a shot by Jimmy Cringan, and in his desperation to stop the loose ball falling to Bradford's feet he palmed it away and then somehow managed to throw it into his own net.

Years later the derby fixture would become fated for Aston Villa goalkeeping blunders. It seemed the tradition that ultimately cursed the likes of Peter Enckelman and Thomas Sorensen could be traced back to the 1920s!

27th February 1926

Division One

Birmingham 2

Briggs (2)

Aston Villa 1

Walker

Attendance: 38,231

BIRMINGHAM: *Tremelling, Womack, Jones, Liddell, Hunter, Dale, Harris, Crosbie, Briggs, Linley, Russell*

ASTON VILLA: *Spiers, Smart, Mort, Corbett, Dr V.E. Milne, G. Blackburn, York, Kirton, Stephenson, Walker, Dorrell*

This was the season when Joe Bradford confirmed his absolute quality. The two that had rescued a point at Villa Park earlier in the season were part of a run of 21 goals in 28 games up until the end of January.

So when he was then ruled out for a few weeks with an injury gained during an FA Cup defeat to South Shields – in which he had also scored a penalty – Birmingham had problems.

In his absence they turned to winger George Briggs to switch to centre-forward, and it proved a smart move.

Briggs, a former coal miner who had been discovered two years earlier playing for Denaby United in the Midland League, and transferred for the sum of £400, had a good scoring record cutting in from wide positions. His eye for a goal and strength made him a natural to lead the line.

He was the most influential player early in this game, and after 17 minutes gave the Blues the lead as he ran on to a clever pass from Ted Linley.

Villa responded well, and Dan Tremelling made a good save from a long-range shot by Dr Milne, but just as they were threatening to get back into the game, they suffered more bad luck when inside-left Billy Walker received a kick on the knee and had to be carried off.

He bravely returned after the interval, and had a header saved by Tremelling.

Villa's defence was attempting to play an offside trap, and it let them down when full-back Tommy Mort thought he'd caught Briggs out and stopped – but the linesman didn't flag.

Goalkeeper Cyril Spiers managed to turn the shot away for a corner, only for his defenders to allow Briggs room for another chance which this time he put away.

Villa did reasonably well but lacked forward power. With Len Capewell missing through injury, his replacement George Stephenson, according to reports at the time, "tried hard but lacked the strength to make an impact."

Even so, Walker reduced the lead with five minutes left, but by then it was too late and the Blues held on to win.

30th October 1926

Division One
Birmingham 1
Crosbie
Aston Villa 2
Dorrell, Walker
Attendance: 48,104
BIRMINGHAM: *Tremelling, Smith, Barton, Liddell, Cringan, Dale, Harris, Crosbie, Briggs, Bradford, Thirlaway*
ASTON VILLA: *Jackson, Bowen, Mort, Kingdon, Dr V.E. Milne, Moss, York, Stephenson, Harris, Walker, Dorrell*

While Birmingham had embraced for some years the "modern" concept of employing a team manager to select the side and dictate tactics, Aston Villa continued their tradition of running the club and picking their team through the directors.

It was a practice that was causing some debate at the start of this campaign as, under the guidance of Billy Beer, the Blues set off winning seven of their first 12 games including a 2-0 win away to champions Huddersfield in which Joe Bradford (who else?) scored twice.

Villa, meanwhile, were stuttering badly and a 2-0 win over West Bromwich Albion the week before was only their third success of the season.

Their run without taking all the points from a game at St Andrew's now stretched back for 19 years, and it looked as if there could be more trouble to come when George Briggs had the ball in the net in the first few minutes, only for it to be disallowed for offside.

Villa got into the game, however, and took the lead on 12 minutes when Billy Walker and Dicky York combined to set up Arthur Dorrell.

Within two minutes Birmingham were level, however. Villa conceded a free-kick for hand ball, and though Tommy Jackson blocked Dicky Dale's hard shot, the ball spun for Johnny Crosbie to force it home.

From there it was nip and tuck, with Walker missing from a free-kick on the edge of the area just before half-time, and then Dr Milne twice clearing off the line after the interval.

George Stephenson, the youngest of three brothers who played for Villa, hesitated over a good chance to take the lead, and it was beginning to look sure to be a draw as Dan Tremelling saved a certain goal from Dorrell with five minutes left.

But then Villa forced one more corner, and in the scramble that followed, Walker stabbed the ball home to send the visiting supporters away celebrating a rare St Andrew's success.

19th March 1927

Division One

Aston Villa 4

Cook, Stephenson, York (2)

Birmingham 2

Bond, Scriven

Attendance: 49,334

ASTON VILLA: *Jackson, Smart, Bowen, Kingdon, Talbot, Moss, York, Kirton, Cook, Stephenson, Dorrell*

BIRMINGHAM: *Tremelling, Womack, Barton, Liddell, Cringan, Dale, Bond, Crosbie, Briggs, Russell, Scriven*

It's funny how some themes keep recurring in these matches – for this was another bad derby day for a goalkeeper.

The culprit this time was Birmingham's Dan Tremelling. Now approaching 30, he had been a stalwart of the club ever since making his debut when League football resumed in 1919 following the First World War.

Tremelling actually went on to win his only England cap later this year – but this particular game was a nightmare for him.

In front of yet another huge crowd in the early spring sunshine, Birmingham had started well and deserved to take the lead after 19 minutes through inside-forward Benny Bond.

He tried a shot that was blocked, and reacted quickest to the loose ball to fire another effort into the corner for his first goal for the club.

Birmingham's goalkeeper couldn't take too much blame for the equalizer shortly afterwards, though. Dicky York's cross from a free-kick reached Arthur Dorrell whose effort rebounded down from the bar to where Billy Cook scored from close range.

But he was at fault as George Stephenson tried an optimistic effort from 25 yards and for some reason the Birmingham goalkeeper made no attempt to stop it as it sailed into the goal.

He was just as stranded when Dorrell hit the crossbar soon afterwards.

Aubrey Scriven brought the scores level with a header soon after half-time, but Tremelling's nightmare continued as he went to catch a Dicky York free-kick but couldn't hold it and the ball dribbled over the line.

The Blues spent a long period looking for another equalizer, but were missing the influence of Joe Bradford who was out injured.

Even when George Briggs was brought down 4 yards from goal, the referee Mr Scholey from Sheffield declined to award a penalty, much to the anger of Birmingham's supporters.

Then came the final goalkeeping calamity. Tremelling and left-half Dicky Dale collided as they both went for the same ball defending a free-kick, leaving York to head into the empty net and the two Birmingham players both needing treatment.

5th November 1927

Division One
Birmingham 1
Crosbie
Aston Villa 1
Walker
Attendance: 47,605
BIRMINGHAM: *Tremelling, Smith, Womack, Dale, Cringan, Leslie, Bond, Crosbie, Bradford, Briggs, Johnson*
ASTON VILLA: *Jackson, Smart, Bowen, Gibson, Dr V.E. Milne, Kingdon, York, Beresford, Cook, Walker, Dorrell*

Average attendances at St Andrew's at the start of the 1927–28 season were less than 20,000 – but when derby day came round in November it was a different matter entirely.

The gates were opened early and the crowds poured in to fill the giant banked terraces.

There was a danger to that, however, and before kick-off a crush barrier at the Railway End of the stadium gave way, and a number of spectators were injured as they tumbled dangerously forward down the steep steps.

There were ambulances and St John's first aid men at work to deal with the casualties, but the game still kicked-off on time and players from both teams entered into a spirited contest.

Birmingham were in a bit of a crisis having won only three matches. There were fears it could be a relegation season, and demands locally to know why they were unable to compete financially with some of the bigger clubs in the First Division.

They did, however, have their talisman Joe Bradford back from injury for this game, and he caused a lot of problems for Villa during a tense but goalless first half.

The Blues took the lead straight after the interval, thanks to yet another derby goalkeeping mistake. Tommy Jackson failed to gather the ball, giving Johnny Crosbie the chance to tap it home.

Villa fought hard to recover, with Dicky York again their danger man on one wing and Arthur Dorrell firing in good crosses from the other.

It was York who made the equalizing goal after 77 minutes, putting the ball into the danger area where centre-half Jimmy Cringan failed to control it and teed up Billy Walker for a simple equalizer.

The Blues could still have found a winner, but Jackson made up for his earlier mistake with a great save from Benny Bond in the final minute.

17th March 1928

Division One

Aston Villa 1

Smart (pen)

Birmingham 1

Bradford

Attendance: 59,367

ASTON VILLA: *Olney, Smart, Mort, Gibson, Dr V.E. Milne, Kingdon,*
York, Cook, Waring, Walker, Dorrell
BIRMINGHAM: *Tremelling, Liddell, Randle, Cringan, Barton, Leslie,*
Briggs, Crosbie, Bradford, Curtis, Ellis

It was a source of frustration for Birmingham supporters that Joe
Bradford was never given more international recognition. Despite
his goalscoring feats with a record 267 League and Cup goals in
445 senior appearances for the club, he was picked only 12 times
for England, despite scoring seven goals in those matches.

It was claimed there was a bias towards the London clubs in the
FA's selection committee, and Bradford had to be content with just
those dozen caps – plus five appearances for the representative
Football League XI which played occasional matches against the
Scottish League.

Bradford had been away on one of those trips the week before,
so was keenly welcomed back to a Birmingham team which was
involved in an uncomfortable scrap against relegation.

It was the Blues who started this game best, forcing Villa keeper
Ben Olney to make an early save from winger Bill Ellis.

With 12 minutes gone Bradford was the hero, scoring the
opening goal after George Briggs had created some space and
skipped away from an attempted tackle by Tommy Mort.

Olney was kept busy, making more saves from both Ellis and
Bradford as Birmingham dominated the remainder of the first half.

After the break the game changed, with Dr Milne setting things
up from centre-half as well as defending stoutly.

But the Blues thought they would hang on to their win until, with
four minutes remaining, came more controversy in a fixture that
was always spiky.

Alec Leslie was deemed to have handled the ball as he tried to
cut out a centre from Billy Kingdon. It was described as a "mysterious
decision", but it stood and full-back Tommy Smart stepped up to

thump the ball beyond the reach of goalkeeper Dan Tremelling.

If Birmingham fans were angry at that, they were furious as in the final minute it appeared that Villa's Jimmy Gibson had also handled in the box, but this time no penalty was awarded and the game finished a draw.

It was tough on the Blues, who had played the better passing football and kept Olney the busier of the two goalkeepers.

27th October 1928

Division One

Birmingham 2

Cringan, Bradford

Aston Villa 4

Waring, Walker (2), Beresford

Attendance: 36,261

BIRMINGHAM: *Hibbs, Liddell, Randle, Dale, Cringan, Leslie, Bond, Crosbie, Briggs, Bradford, Hicks*

ASTON VILLA: *Olney, Smart, Bowen, Kingdon, Dr V.E. Milne, Tate, York, Beresford, Waring, Walker, Dorrell*

Heavy rain was falling on St Andrew's with puddles on parts of the pitch – a blow for Birmingham who were parading record signing George Hicks on his debut after joining from Manchester City.

The left-winger had been part of the City side which had won the Second Division title the year before and his arrival was intended to help provide more ammunition for Joe Bradford's continued goalscoring spree.

But it was Villa who took the lead after just three minutes when Billy Kingdon began an attack that ended with Tom "Pongo" Waring firing in a hard, straight shot.

The speed of winger Dicky York was causing problems for Blues full-back Jack Randle, but it was the home team which came up with an equalizer – one more for the list of derby goalkeeping blunders as Ben Olney got hands to Jimmy Cringan's 20-yard shot but couldn't stop it squirming across the line.

That swung the momentum of the game, and Benny Bond combined with Johnny Crosbie to create a chance for Bradford to put the Blues in front at half-time.

Birmingham continued to dominate, until, against the run of play, a centre from Joe Beresford found Billy Walker unmarked for an equalizer.

The rain had eased but it was now misty and visibility was poor. Birmingham were handicapped when Billy Liddell was hurt in a tackle and became a passenger at outside-right. Walker missed an easy chance before, with 13 minutes left, Beresford gave Villa the lead, forcing the ball home from the third of three corners in quick succession.

It was from another corner, five minutes from the end, that Walker got Villa's fourth goal to make the victory safe.

9th March 1929

Division One

Aston Villa 1

Waring

Birmingham 2

Mills, Crosbie

Attendance: 56,528

ASTON VILLA: *Olney, Smart, Mort, Gibson, Talbot, Tate, York, Beresford, Waring, Walker, Dorrell*

BIRMINGHAM: *Hibbs, Barkas, Randle, Liddell, Morrall, Leslie, Briggs, Crosbie, Mills, Bradford, Hicks*

The Blues had begun this season under a new manager – Leslie Knighton – who had brought new ambition and drive to St Andrew's.

His own playing career at lower levels had been cut short by injury, but he had thrown himself into coaching with such enthusiasm that at the age of just 25 he had a brief spell as caretaker manager of Huddersfield – and was still just 32 when appointed manager of Arsenal.

What should have been the big job didn't quite work out, however, as the Gunners chairman Sir Henry Norris refused to back his transfer plans, putting a cap of £1,000 on any fee. After losing his job in 1925 he spent three years at Bournemouth before the Blues gave him his big chance.

It proved an inspired appointment as he built the team which would give the club some of its best years in the 1930s.

Not all of his signings worked out, however. Bert "Paddy" Mills came from Notts County with a record of a goal every two games and went straight into the side.

A strong forward, the goal he scored in the first half of this game was his third in five matches following his debut and Blues fans were expecting big things.

Sadly it also proved to be his last goal in a Birmingham shirt. He failed to settle, and the following season, having played just 13 games in all, was sold to Hull where his career had begun.

In a tight contest, watched by Villa's biggest crowd of the season, Pongo Waring had an early effort ruled out for offside but there was nothing wrong when George Dorrell played a pass for him to score after 15 minutes.

The Blues were level within 60 seconds, as Ben Olney failed to hold Joe Bradford's shot and Mills forced the loose ball home.

Olney was then to blame for the winner, as Johnny Crosbie tried an optimistic shot which the goalkeeper looked to have covered, only for the ball to squirm underneath him and into the net.

It proved to be a significant defeat for Villa. They also lost their next two League matches and were then knocked out of the FA Cup in the semi-finals. Despite a late rally they finished the season two points behind champions Sheffield Wednesday.

31ˢᵗ August 1929

Division One

Aston Villa 2

Chester, York

Birmingham 1

Bradford

Attendance: 36,834

ASTON VILLA: *Olney, Smart, Mort, Kingdon, Gibson, Tate, York, Brown, Waring, Walker, Chester*

BIRMINGHAM: *Hibbs, Barkas, Randle, Liddell, Cringan, Blyth, Bond, Crosbie, Bradford, Briggs, Hicks*

The summer of 1929 was Aston Villa's turn to show ambition, signing England centre-forward George Brown from Huddersfield Town.

Aged 26, he had been discovered by the Yorkshire club playing for his pit team at Mickley and then enjoyed phenomenal success.

He had scored 142 goals in 213 League games, and a further 17 from 16 FA Cup matches. With Tom "Pongo" Waring having hit 25 League goals the previous season, and Billy Walker still at the peak of his powers, spending a £5,000 transfer fee to sign Brown gave Villa a dream forward line.

The opening day of the season saw them teamed together for the first time – but bizarrely it was the wingers who actually got the goals to start the season with a win.

With thunderstorms swirling around Villa Park, Reg Chester ran on to a neat pass by Walker to open the scoring after 11 minutes.

Birmingham, who were also parading a new signing in former Arsenal captain Bill Blyth, fought back and got an equalizer before the break when Joe Bradford headed home a Johnny Crosbie centre.

That, incidentally, was the start of an astonishing sequence of 14 goals in the first eight games of the season including three hat-tricks. (He also scored five in one game for the Football League against the Irish League during that spell).

But an injury to George Briggs swung the game back in Villa's favour, and it was the pace of Dicky York which again proved Birmingham's undoing as six minutes after the break he cut in from the right to hit a powerful shot that Harry Hibbs couldn't reach.

Hibbs had to make another good save from George Brown, and Pongo Waring hit the post as Villa dominated the final stages of the game and could have won by more.

28th December 1929

Division One

Birmingham 1

Crosbie

Aston Villa 1

Walker

Attendance: 33,228

BIRMINGHAM: *Hibbs, Liddell, Barkas, Firth, Morrall, Leslie, Curtis, Crosbie, Haywood, Briggs, Hicks*

ASTON VILLA: *Olney, Bowen, Mort, Kingdon, Talbot, Tate, York, Waring, Brown, Walker, Dorrell*

The Villa supporters who made their way to St Andrew's didn't realize it, but they were seeing a little piece of club history a couple of days before celebrating the dawn of a new decade.

This turned out to be the final appearance of the 390 made by left-winger Arthur Dorrell.

The son of Billy Dorrell, who played for Villa in the 1890s, Arthur had joined the club straight after finishing Army service during the First World War and was pretty much a fixture on the left wing all through the 1920s.

At the age of 33, however, he had missed the first part of this campaign through injury and Reg Chester was handed the number 11 shirt. Dorrell finally got back into the side for the Christmas Day and Boxing Day games against Manchester City, and then stayed in for the short trip for the derby.

It was a disappointing performance by the whole team, however. Rain that followed an overnight frost made the pitch treacherous, and the slippery conditions caused a lot of mistakes by both sides.

Just to make matters worse it began to pour down during the game turning the pitch to heavy mud, and Villa's attempts to play their normal passing game were confounded by the conditions.

Even so they took the lead in the 73rd minute with Billy Walker heading in a Dorrell corner.

But eight minutes from the end Johnny Crosbie, the one man able to make light of the conditions with his balance and skill, found some space for an equalizer.

Despite his corner having made Villa's goal, Dorrell was not chosen for the team that met Leeds a few days later, when it was decided to give a teenager called Eric Houghton his chance – the one who went on to play for the club for two decades and later become its manager!

The Blues were chopping and changing at this time as Leslie Knighton put together the team which was to reach the FA Cup final the following season. The side showed five changes from the one which had begun the season at Villa Park back in August.

Chapter Four

The 1930s

Great clubs need great heroes, and few have been as charismatic as Aston Villa's hero of the 1930s, centre-forward Tom "Pongo" Waring.

He actually arrived at the club in February of 1928, a raw 21-year-old who had made headlines scoring goals for Tranmere in the Third Division North. Villa had to beat off competition from Arsenal, Bolton and Manchester United to secure his signature for a £4,700 transfer fee. His nickname, after a popular cartoon character of the time and given because of his reputation as a joker, added to the romance. His arrival caused such excitement that a crowd of 23,600 turned up at a reserve team game – oddly enough against Birmingham – to see him make his debut. He didn't disappoint any of them, scoring a first-half hat-trick.

From there the goals just kept flowing, 32 in his first full season, 36 in the next, and then the astonishing campaign of 1930–31 when he rattled in 50 in 40 appearances – 49 of them in his 39 First Division appearances. It was a swashbuckling year in which Villa scored 128 League goals, a record which remains unmatched. Incredibly it earned only second place in the table, however, as Arsenal scored 127 but let in considerably fewer!

It was an exciting and successful time on both sides of the city. While Villa were firing in the League, Birmingham had their best campaign in the FA Cup, as Joe Bradford scored in every round to take them to their first final. Sadly both clubs ended up just missing out on silverware, however.

The Blues were red-hot favourites against West Bromwich Albion. Torrential rain turned the pitch into a mudbath, however, which helped their Second Division opponents, and though Bradford scored to equalize a first-half goal, they let in a winner within a minute.

Villa were runners-up again in 1933, and responded to another disappointment by breaking years of tradition and appointing their first team manager in James McMullan. A former Scotland international, he was considered to have all the qualities needed, and he showed his ambition by breaking the British transfer record to sign Jimmy Allen from Portsmouth for £10,775.

Unhappily the promises came to nothing. Instead of taking the team to new heights they ended up breaking ground in the opposite direction, and by the time he was relieved of his responsibilities in October 1935 it was too late to prevent Villa getting relegated for the first time in their history. It didn't help that Pongo Waring demanded a transfer in protest at McMullan's dismissal.

Villa's answer was to appoint Jimmy Hogan, who was years ahead of his time as a coach who had worked in Switzerland and Austria. He put the club back together, and took the Second Division by storm in 1938 before finishing a respectable 12th the following year. Sadly the onset of the Second World War meant Villa fans would never get to know what he might have achieved.

Meanwhile Birmingham had also seen their hopes fade in the middle of the decade as the 1931 FA Cup final side grew old together. Leslie Knighton left to take a lucrative job in charge of Chelsea and his successor George Liddell, who had played nearly 350 games for the Blues, found stepping up to management difficult.

He fought and won a couple of relegation fights, and believed he was beginning to put a new and more successful team together as they drew a record 18 times in the 1937–38 season. Instead the draws turned to defeats and Birmingham finished 21st in 1939 to lose their top-flight status for the first time in nearly two decades.

Record in the 1930s

Aston Villa:

Season	League	P	W	D	L	F	A	Pts	Position
1930–31	Div 1	42	25	9	8	128	76	59	2
1931–32	Div 1	42	19	8	15	104	72	46	5
1932–33	Div 1	42	23	8	11	92	67	54	2
1933–34	Div 1	42	14	12	16	78	75	40	13
1934–35	Div 1	42	14	13	15	74	88	41	13
1935–36	Div 1	42	13	9	20	81	110	35	21
1936–37	Div 2	42	16	12	14	82	70	44	9
1937–38	Div 2	42	25	7	10	73	35	57	1
1938–39	Div 1	42	16	9	17	71	60	41	12

FA Cup

1930–31	2-2, 1-3 v Arsenal (third round)
1931–32	1-1, 0-1 v Portsmouth (fourth round)
1932–33	0-3 v Sunderland (fourth round)
1933–34	1-6 v Manchester City (semi-final)
1934–35	1-3 v Bradford City (third round)
1935–36	0-1 v Huddersfield Town (third round)
1936–37	2-3 v Burnley (third round)
1937–38	1-2 v Preston North End (semi-final)
1938–39	0-2 v Preston North End (fourth round)

Birmingham:

Season	League	P	W	D	L	F	A	Pts	Position
1930–31	Div 1	42	13	10	19	55	70	36	19
1931–32	Div 1	42	18	8	16	78	67	44	9
1932–33	Div 1	42	14	11	17	57	57	39	13
1933–34	Div 1	42	12	12	18	54	56	36	20
1934–35	Div 1	42	13	10	19	63	81	36	19
1935–36	Div 1	42	15	11	16	61	63	41	12

1936–37	Div 1	42	13	15	14	64	60	41	11
1937–38	Div 1	42	10	18	14	58	62	38	18
1938–39	Div 1	42	12	8	22	62	84	32	21

FA Cup

1930–31	1-2 v West Bromwich Albion (final at Wembley)
1931–32	1-2 v Grimsby (fourth round)
1932–33	0-4 v West Ham (sixth round)
1933–34	1-2 v Leicester City (fifth round)
1934–35	2-3 v Burnley (sixth round)
1935–36	0-2 v Barnsley (fourth round)
1936–37	1-4 v Stoke City (third round)
1937–38	0-1 v Blackpool (third round)
1938–39	2-2, 1-2 v Everton (fifth round)

18th October 1930

Division One

Aston Villa 1

Waring

Birmingham 1

Briggs

Attendance: 55,482

ASTON VILLA: *Biddlestone, Bowen, Mort, Gibson, Talbot, Tate, Mandley, Brown, Waring, Walker, Houghton*

BIRMINGHAM: *Hibbs, Liddell, Barkas, Cringan, Morrall, Leslie, Horsman, Crosbie, Briggs, Bradford, Curtis*

This was the season when Villa's forwards clicked into the most successful spell of their history – an incredible 128 goals scored in a single First Division campaign, not only the club record but still the best achieved by any team in a top-flight season.

Pongo Waring was the man who was at the forefront of it all, scoring in each of the first seven League matches by which time he had already amassed a total of 13 goals. Waring was to finish the season with a remarkable tally of 50 in all competitions, all but one of them scored in the First Division, while Eric Houghton collected 30 in his 41 matches.

The Blues were also on a hot streak in front of goal, with 17 shared around the team during their opening 10 matches, and the huge crowd which filled Villa Park were expecting to see lots of goals.

It looked as if they would not be disappointed when with 25 minutes gone Joe Bradford used clever footwork to get away from Jimmy Gibson, and played a slide rule pass that drew Fred Biddlestone out of his goal just a fraction too late to leave George Briggs the simplest of chances.

The Blues poured forward looking for a second, but 10 minutes before half-time a long clearance by Joe Tate aimed at easing the pressure was fortunate to find Jack Mandley.

His centre looked harmless until Harry Hibbs came out to deal with it and collided with George Liddell, leaving Pongo Waring a simple chance to put the ball in the net with both of them lying on the floor.

Hibbs, who had made his England debut the previous season and was becoming established as his country's first choice goalkeeper, redeemed himself with some good saves after the break as – with Crosbie a passenger on the wing after collecting an injury – Villa dominated the game but couldn't find a winner.

21st February 1931

Division One
Birmingham 0
Aston Villa 4
Tate, Mandley, Houghton, Beresford
Attendance: 49,609
BIRMINGHAM: *Hibbs, Liddell, Randle, Cringan, Fillingham, Firth, Horsman, Briggs, Bradford, Gregg, Curtis*

ASTON VILLA: R. *Miles, Smart, Mort, Gibson, Talbot, Tate, Mandley, Beresford, Waring, Walker, Houghton*

Birmingham were hitting form in the second half of the season, and with Joe Bradford scoring freely had looked impressive as their FA Cup run got under way.

They had won against Liverpool at Anfield in the third round before knocking out Port Vale and Watford, and had also just scored impressive wins over Blackburn and Blackpool in the League.

But bad luck struck them ahead of the clash with Villa as a 'flu bug went through their camp. It ruled out Ned Barkas, Alec Leslie and George Morrall – and if that wasn't bad enough Johnny Crosbie was also sidelined by an ankle injury.

Free-scoring Villa were in just the mood to take advantage of playing weakened opposition, and took the lead after 25 minutes. Right-winger Jack Mandley put over a cross, and in a scramble it fell to Joe Tate, unmarked just outside the penalty area, who scored with a first-time shot.

Blues put up a brave fightback, and goalkeeper Reg Miles cleared off the line from Joe Bradford before then producing a brilliant save to deny the same player. Just before the break left-winger Ernie Curtis shot over the bar from close range.

But with 58 minutes gone Villa got a second goal from a Pongo Waring shot that Harry Hibbs could only palm into the path of Jack Mandley.

Then Mandley himself went on a dangerous run down the right before floating over a perfectly judged centre that Eric Houghton headed home.

With 10 minutes to go Villa got the best of their four goals, with Waring running out wide to create space before driving over another cross for Joe Beresford to head beyond Hibbs' reach.

21ˢᵗ November 1931

Division One

Aston Villa 3

Walker, Waring (2)

Birmingham 2

Smith (2)

Attendance: 44,948

ASTON VILLA: *Biddlestone, Smart, Mort, Wood, Talbot, Tate, Mandley, Beresford, Waring, Walker, Houghton*

BIRMINGHAM: *Hibbs, Liddell, Barkas, Stoker, Morrall, Cringan, Briggs, Grosvenor, Smith, Gregg, Curtis*

Joe Bradford had become something of a talisman for Birmingham in these derby games – so it came as a huge blow for manager Leslie Knighton when his centre-forward failed a fitness test.

He had scored in every round of the trip to the FA Cup final the previous season, and already had a dozen goals in this campaign.

Knighton took a gamble by picking untried youngster Samuel Smith at centre-forward. The Pelsall-born player had recently been purchased from local club Walsall L.M.S. – and he justified his decision by scoring both goals and proving an able replacement for Bradford.

Ironically, however, it was keeping goals out rather than scoring them that proved to be Birmingham's problem as Villa went 2-0 up at half-time.

Billy Walker got the first after just five minutes following a fine run and centre by Eric Houghton, and though there followed a period of Blues pressure in the search for an equalizer, with full-backs Tommy Smart and Tommy Mort having to play well to keep them at bay, the second goal came on 37 minutes.

Walker and Houghton were involved again, combining well to set up a chance for Pongo Waring who shook off George Liddell's tackle as he shot beyond the reach of Harry Hibbs.

Smith looked like being the game's hero, however, as two minutes after the break he got onto a centre from Ernie Curtis to head home, and then reacted quickest to grab a 61st-minute equalizer when Fred Biddlestone failed to hold a Jimmy Cringan shot.

But the Blues' joy didn't last long. A clever pass by Tommy Wood saw Waring race through and put the ball out of Hibbs' reach.

Waring might have had another but for a brilliant save by Hibbs, but despite mounting late attacks the Blues couldn't find another equalizer.

2nd April 1932

Division One

Birmingham 1

Smith

Aston Villa 1

Houghton

Attendance: 35,671

BIRMINGHAM: *Hibbs, Liddell, Cringan, Stoker, Morrall, Fillingham, Briggs, Grosvenor, Smith, Bradford, Curtis*

ASTON VILLA: *Morton, Blair, Mort, Gibson, Talbot, Tate, Mandley, Brown, Waring, Astley, Houghton*

This was a good season for the Blues, and they ended up in ninth place in the table – but were suffering one of those mysterious "blips" as they went into this game.

A 5-1 thrashing at Bolton Wanderers in early March had been the first of five defeats in a row – the worst of them another five-goal hammering at home to Manchester City a week earlier.

Goalkeeper Jimmy Mittell had been blamed for at least two of those, and Birmingham were glad to have the imposing figure of Harry Hibbs back from injury to replace him.

Ironically though, Hibbs suffered an early attack of the jitters, slipping as he tried to deal with a centre from Jack Mandley with 11 minutes gone and the ball fell for Eric Houghton to score.

It was tough on the Blues, who had actually opened the game well, with Joe Bradford unlucky to see a good attempt hit the post.

They responded well to the setback with Scottish full-back Danny Blair having to make a couple of vital interceptions, while Bradford hit a free-kick from the edge of the area into Villa's defensive wall.

It was Bradford who set up Birmingham's equalizer after 34 minutes, beating two defenders before squaring the ball to give Samuel Smith an easy finish.

The second half was even, with the biggest scare for either side coming when Hibbs made yet another handling mistake and dropped a free-kick that was fired straight at him. Fortunately he managed to recover and dive on the ball before a Villa forward could take advantage.

22nd October 1932

Division One

Aston Villa 1

Houghton

Birmingham 0

Attendance: 52,191

ASTON VILLA: *Morton, Blair, Mort, Gibson, Talbot, Tate, Mandley, Astley, Brown, Walker, Houghton*

BIRMINGHAM: *Hibbs, Booton, Smith, Stoker, Morrall, Fillingham, Briggs, Grosvenor, Bradford, Gregg, Thorogood*

This victory marked Villa's best start to a top-flight season, an unbeaten run of 11 games which would not be bettered until 66 years later when John Gregory's side won at Southampton to notch up their 12th game without defeat.

As derby day dawned in 1932, however, all the talk was about whether this Villa team were going to be good enough to win the title with seven wins and three draws from their opening matches and Arsenal trailing behind them in the table.

Heavy rain had left the Villa Park pitch soaked, and on the slick surface Villa's passing game was effective.

Eric Houghton hit the bar with an early free-kick, and inside-forward Dai Astley had a goal disallowed for a debatable offside decision, while Harry Hibbs showed why he was now firmly established as England's goalkeeper with an outstanding display.

Birmingham, despite having Joe Bradford back from injury, had little to offer going forward although goalkeeper Harry Morton did have to tip over a long-range shot from George Morrall.

There were 59 minutes gone when Villa finally got the breakthrough thanks to a superb effort by Houghton.

He began the move with a clever pass to George Brown on the left, and when he received a return pass he evaded left-back Bernard Smith before beating Hibbs with a superb shot from 20 yards.

Jack Thorogood hit the post on 75 minutes as Birmingham tried to respond, but with Bradford clearly not fully fit and lacking confidence, the Blues couldn't muster another serious challenge.

8th March 1933

Division One

Birmingham 3

Briggs, Bradford, Grosvenor

Aston Villa 2

Brown, Mandley

Attendance: 24,868

ASTON VILLA: *Morton, Blair, Mort, Gibson, Callaghan, Simpson, Mandley, Astley, Brown, Walker, Houghton*

BIRMINGHAM: *Hibbs, Booton, Barkas, Stoker, Morrall, Calladine, Briggs, Grosvenor, Bradford, Gregg, Curtis*

Joe Bradford's place in Birmingham's history was secure by this time – he had overtaken Steve Bloomer's scoring record of 232 goals back on Christmas Eve with the first of two against Portsmouth.

An injury then forced him to miss half a dozen games, but if there was one match he was determined to be fit again for, it was when Villa came to St Andrew's.

He marked his return with a superb display – and not just by scoring the second of two goals either side of half-time which put the Blues in charge of the match.

The *Daily Mirror* report of the day describes it as a complete centre-forward's performance, holding the ball when it was played forward down the middle of the pitch and also passing it cleverly.

"Some of Birmingham's bouts of passing were remarkably skilful – indeed, one scarcely remembers the home side playing cleverer football. They fairly outshone the Villa in this important part of the game," says the report.

George Brown did give Villa some hope with a goal to make it 2-1, but the Blues deserved to restore a two-goal advantage thanks to Tom Grosvenor, and another Villa effort from Jack Mandley was scant consolation for a poor performance from the visitors.

2nd December 1933

Division One
Birmingham 0
Aston Villa 0
Attendance: 34,718
BIRMINGHAM: *Hibbs, Booton, Fillingham, Stoker, Morrall, Calladine, Horsman, Grosvenor, Bradford, Roberts, White*
ASTON VILLA: *Morton, Mort, Blair, Simpson, Talbot, Kingdon, Cunliffe, Astley, Waring, Beresford, Houghton*

The Blues had suffered upheaval during the summer when manager Leslie Knighton, who had built a team that had become established in the First Division, as well as guiding them to the 1931 FA Cup final, received an offer to take over Chelsea.

It was a lucrative opportunity that he could not resist, and the response of chairman Harry Morris was to put former player George Liddell in charge.

Liddell had been ambitious to become a manager throughout the later stages of his playing career, and Mr Morris offered the opinion that "George will do a good job, just like he did as a player."

He didn't find it so easy, however, and had won only four matches by the time Villa arrived at St Andrew's on a cold December Saturday.

With his 33rd birthday approaching, centre-forward Joe Bradford had begun to pass the peak of his powers and had scored just four goals in the club's first 16 games.

He was strangely quiet again as Villa's defence with Tommy Mort playing well was largely untroubled in what became an unusually dull derby contest – only the third goalless draw in the 44 competitive matches between the teams.

14th April 1934

Division One
Aston Villa 1
Dix
Birmingham 1
Calladine
Attendance: 34,196
ASTON VILLA: *Morton, Blair, Nibloe, Gardner, Gibson, Kingdon, Houghton, Brocklebank, Astley, Dix, Cunliffe*
BIRMINGHAM: *Clack, Booton, Barkas, Lea, Morrall, Calladine, Moffat, Roberts, Fillingham, Bradford, Guest*

George Liddell's first season in charge had gone from bad to worse, with a run of just one win in 14 matches through the depths of winter. He chopped and changed the team in search of solutions, ending up using 29 players in all during the campaign, a number almost unheard of in the days when no substitutes were allowed.

At one stage the Blues were buried in the relegation zone, but by mid-April were beginning to mount a survival campaign winning three of their previous five matches before the visit to Villa Park.

Villa were also going through a transitional period, with Billy Walker having played the last of his 531 games for the club earlier in the season. And it didn't help them that their new goalscorer Pongo Waring was injured for the last couple of months of the season.

Welshman Dai Astley took over centre-forward duties in his absence, and set up a goal for Bristol-born Ronnie Dix after only three minutes.

Centre-half Jimmy Gibson started the movement, with a pass to Dix who tried to set up Astley, but when the centre-forward was tackled he pushed the ball back and Dix, with a clear view of goal, struck a low shot that found the bottom corner.

Terry Morrall might have equalized while Bob Brocklebank missed a good chance to increase the lead, but the Blues began to get back into the game and drew level after 34 minutes.

Outside-right Sid Moffat found some room to fire over a cross that found centre-half Charlie Calladine – who had gone up for a corner and not returned to his normal defensive duties – in some space to tap the ball home from close range. It was his first League goal of the season, and it could have set up a victory, but Billy Guest missed a golden chance in the second half.

25th August 1934

Division One

Birmingham 2

Harris, Guest

Aston Villa 1

Waring

Attendance: 53,930

BIRMINGHAM: *Hibbs, Booton, Hubbard, Stoker, Morrall, Calladine, Moffat, Harris, Mangnall, Bradford, Guest*

ASTON VILLA: *Morton, Beeson, Mort, Gardner, Allen, Gibson, Houghton, Astley, Waring, Dix, Cunliffe*

After escaping relegation by just two points, Birmingham had a summer to regroup and began the new campaign in buoyant mood.

They had created a new supporters' club during the summer, and before the opening game at St Andrew's they paraded a whippet called Peggy who was to be their new mascot and had been made the first honorary member of the newly formed organization.

The stunt built up the atmosphere and the Blues players responded to the new enthusiasm, with Joe Bradford and Billy Guest causing problems early on.

Villa had paid a British record transfer fee of £10,775 to sign centre-half Jimmy Allen from Portsmouth but he was being given a tough debut – as was right-back George Beeson who was also making his first appearance after being signed from Sheffield Wednesday.

The Blues goalkeeper Harry Hibbs had to make a save from Pongo Waring, but it was mostly one-way traffic and the home team thought they had scored after 29 minutes when Fred Harris forced the ball home. Unfortunately it was disallowed because Guest had fouled Beeson before setting up the chance.

The St Andrew's fans didn't have more than a minute to wait, however, as Harris pounced on the loose ball after Harry Morton saved Dave Mangnall's shot but couldn't hold the ball.

Villa were missing injured captain Danny Blair, who had been hurt in a trial game a week earlier, although they did make a spirited start to the second half.

But the skipper's absence proved crucial as with 51 minutes gone Bradford ran to the corner flag before crossing for Guest to head home.

Waring gave Villa slight hope with a shot from the edge of the area three minutes from the end, but it was too little, too late.

29ᵗʰ December 1934

Division One

Aston Villa 2

Astley, Waring

Birmingham 2

Mangnall (2)

Attendance: 40,785

ASTON VILLA: *Morton, Beeson, Blair, Gardner, Talbot, Kingdon, Houghton, Brocklebank, Waring, Astley, Chester*

BIRMINGHAM: *Hibbs, Booton, Barkas, Lea, Fillingham, Calladine, White, Harris, Mangnall, Bradford, Guest*

This had been a historic season for Villa, the first time they had appointed a team manager after more than 50 years of running the playing side of the club by committee.

Former Scottish international James McMullan was the man entrusted with the responsibility. Aged 39, he had played in two FA Cup finals for Manchester City and was captain of the Scotland "Wembley Wizards" side which had beaten England 5-1 in 1928.

The directors unveiled him in their match programme notes as: "A cool, calculating team manager who knows his football from A to Z – not as a theorist but because of a hard practical experience of many years."

Unfortunately he didn't live up to that billing as he found his feet in management and when Birmingham arrived at Villa Park for this derby fixture was struggling in a run of six games in December with only two draws to show for them. His team had also lost both away and at home to Chelsea in the Christmas Day/Boxing Day double-header.

Heavy rain had pounded Villa Park, and the pitch had to be rolled and covered in sand to allow the game to go ahead. Those conditions were to blame for Blues taking the lead after just five minutes, when a shot from Fred Harris stuck in the mud, handing a simple chance to Dave Mangnall.

Villa dominated from there but struggled to make it count, bringing no more than a couple of easy saves out of Harry Hibbs – then with 33 minutes gone Mangnall got his second, running on to Joe Bradford's pass with Harry Morton too slow to react.

Almost immediately Dai Astley pulled a goal back, and had a bit of luck when a Bradford goal just before half-time was disallowed because Mangnall had fouled Morton.

The conditions underfoot were becoming heavier, but Pongo Waring defied them with a brilliant solo run, getting away from two defenders before going round Hibbs to equalize. Villa held on to the point as Morton made a save in the last minute to stop Mangnall from getting his hat-trick.

23rd November 1935

Division One
Birmingham 2
Jones (2)
Aston Villa 2
Astley (2)
Attendance: **59,971**
BIRMINGHAM: *Hibbs, Booton, Barkas, Stoker, Fillingham, Loughran, White, Grosvenor, Jones, Harris, Guest*
ASTON VILLA: *Morton, Young, Cummings, Gardner, Griffiths, Wood, Houghton, Astley, Palethorpe, Dix, Drinkwater*

Villa's faith in James McMullan's ability as a manager proved seriously misplaced. Two months into the new season he left the club and Frank Barson was appointed coach.

The split came a couple of weeks after Tom "Pongo" Waring had been left out of a side that was thrashed 7-0 at home to West Brom, and just to add to Villa's woes the centre-forward handed in a transfer request. By the time Villa travelled to St Andrew's at the end of November there were only four players still in the team from the side that had played at home to Sheffield Wednesday on the opening day of the campaign back in August.

In contrast Birmingham were enjoying a positive spell, and a record crowd forced their way onto the St Andrew's terraces in the hope of seeing a home win.

By the time the match kicked off, the gates had been closed with more people locked outside, and the crush on the Railway End was such that a number of spectators were hurt. The *Birmingham Sports Argus* report describes the St John Ambulance service having to work hard to deal with the casualties, while many fans spilled on to the track around the pitch to find somewhere to watch the match in comparative safety.

With nine minutes gone Villa took the lead. Ned Barkas failed to get any distance on a clearance, and Dai Astley picked up the loose ball and created some space for himself before scoring with a fine shot from 20 yards.

The Blues quickly drew level from a corner, however, Fred Harris heading the ball to Fred Jones who turned it into the roof of the net from close range.

With 24 minutes gone Villa were in front again – Eric Houghton's centre was cleared by Harry Booton, but the ball went direct to Astley who fired another first-time shot.

It was a sweet moment for Villa captain Astley who had been out of form with only three goals all season up until this game.

But any hope that it might bring a badly needed victory had gone within six minutes, as Lew Stoker won the ball in midfield and supplied a chance for Jones to equalize.

The second half was a thriller – described as "firework football" – but neither team could come up with a winning goal.

28th March 1936

Division One

Aston Villa 2

Hughes (og), Broome

Birmingham 1

Fillingham

Attendance: 49,531

ASTON VILLA: *Biddlestone, Griffiths, Cummings, Massie, Callaghan, Wood, Phillips, Hodgson, Broome, Astley, Houghton*

BIRMINGHAM: *Hibbs, Trigg, Hughes, Stoker, Fillingham, Sykes, Jennings, Devine, Jones, Harris, Guest*

Three wins in five games had set Birmingham up nicely for the chance to achieve a top half of the table finish for the first time in four years, but bad luck struck manager George Liddell on derby day.

His first-choice full-backs Ned Barkas and Billy Steel both suffered from a bout of tonsillitis, forcing him to bring two teenagers into the side. Cyril Trigg and William Hughes had a combined age of 35 and so became the youngest pair of backs to appear in any Football League game up until this time.

The two teenagers did well – especially Trigg – who was making his debut after joining from Bedworth at the start of the season. Villa's threat in the first half was limited to a shot by right-winger Charlie Phillips which beat Harry Hibbs but went wide.

But with 58 minutes gone Eric Houghton combined with Frank Broome to set up a chance from which Broome scored with a hard shot from just inside the area – although the goal was later officially, and harshly for the teenager, recorded as an own goal as the shot deflected off Hughes as he tried to keep it out of the net.

Broome, aged just 20, then put Villa two ahead after 69 minutes as he scored from close range after good work from Gordon Hodgson.

But what should have been a comfortable win from there

became a nervy affair as Villa conceded a needless corner from which Tom Fillingham scored after 76 minutes.

Fred Jones had to go off injured, but even with 10 men, the Blues were still full of fire in the closing stages and Fred Biddlestone pulled off a great save to keep out Joe Devine.

It was an important win for Villa who were second from bottom of the table and fighting for survival just two points behind Chelsea, Grimsby and Leeds. They climbed out of the danger zone with subsequent victories over both West Brom and Wolves.

Sadly, however, it was not enough. A 4-2 defeat to Blackburn on the final day saw the club slip out of the top division for the first time in their history.

29th October 1938

Division One
Birmingham 3
Harris (2), Brown
Aston Villa 0
Attendance: 55,301
BIRMINGHAM: *Clack, Trigg, Hughes, Dearson, Halsall, Richards, White, Jennings, Phillips, Harris, J. Brown*
ASTON VILLA: *Biddlestone, Callaghan, Cummings, Massie, Allen, Iverson, Broome, Haycock, Shell, Starling, Houghton*

In the wake of relegation Villa's directors had shown great foresight in their choice of a new manager, appointing 54-year-old Lancastrian Jimmy Hogan. After ending his playing career at Bolton he had enjoyed considerable success coaching in both Switzerland and Austria, including a spell in which he took the Austrian national team to the 1936 Olympic final shortly before being appointed at Villa Park.

It took him two seasons to bring Villa back to the First Division, but they arrived as champions and had made a respectable start to life in the top flight by the time they travelled to St Andrew's to resume the traditional derby "hostilities".

By now Cyril Trigg and Billy Hughes had established themselves as the Blues' first-choice full-back pairing, and with Harry Hibbs still at the peak of his powers, the home team were stronger in the first half, forcing Villa keeper Fred Biddlestone to make some good saves.

With 62 minutes gone the pressure finally told, however, as Villa's defenders failed to clear a cross by Dai Richards, and Fred Harris took advantage when Biddlestone was slow to come off his line.

Harris had another goal ruled out for offside, but with 75 minutes gone the result was sealed by a goalkeeping blunder. Jackie Brown got away on the left but his cross looked harmless until Biddlestone turned it into his own net.

Villa were overrun from there, with Eric Houghton forced to play in defence because of an injury to Bob Iverson, and Harris headed home his second goal six minutes from the end.

4ᵗʰ March 1939

Division One

Aston Villa 5

Martin (3), Houghton (2, inc. 1 pen)

Birmingham 1

Dearson

Attendance: **40,874**

ASTON VILLA: *Rutherford, Callaghan, Cummings, Massie, Allen, Iverson, Broome, Martin, O'Donnell, Haycock, Houghton*

BIRMINGHAM: *Clack, Trigg, Hughes, Dearson, Halsall, J. Shaw, Jennings, Craven, Jones, Harris, Brown*

It may well have been the defeat at St Andrew's which convinced Villa manager James Hogan that he needed to strengthen his attacking options if the club were to thrive after their return to the top flight.

Little more than a week later he paid Blackpool £10,500 to sign centre-forward Frank O'Donnell and it proved an inspired move.

The Scot, who had built a reputation as a powerful goalscorer with both Celtic and Preston, settled immediately into the team and ended up with 14 goals from 29 games as Villa began to climb the table.

Birmingham, meanwhile, were struggling, despite the brief boost of an FA Cup run which brought a record crowd of more than 67,000 to St Andrew's, paying gate receipts of £4,556, to see them meet Everton in the fifth round.

Manager George Liddell tried to shake things up by signing John Shaw from Grimsby and the left-half made his debut in this game.

Heavy rain in the morning left the pitch heavy, but Villa defied the conditions to take the lead after 17 minutes with a neat passing move, as Eric Houghton and Frank Broome combined to set up Jackie Martin, the inside-right tucking the ball beyond Frank Clack as he came out of goal.

Houghton then made it two with 24 minutes gone, scoring from a narrow angle with a shot that deflected off Don Dearson.

From there Villa took control, although it took them until the 71st minute to get a third when Martin worked his way across from the left wing to score. He completed a hat-trick shortly afterwards with a header and then Houghton, who had hit the bar with a fierce shot, completed the rout from the penalty spot after O'Donnell was fouled by Cyril Trigg.

Dearson got a consolation goal in the final minute for the Blues, but it was to prove a critical defeat as they took only four points from the next seven matches and were doomed to relegation.

Chapter Five

The 1940s and '50s

It was a time of austerity as Britain emerged from the Second World War. Just as football had been one of the things which helped boost the country's morale after the 1914–18 conflict, so another generation flocked to escape their lives for 90 minutes on the terraces every Saturday.

For Aston Villa it was a whole new beginning. Six years after their side had shown so much promise, new manager Alex Massie was having to go back to absolute basics to get a team up and running. He even held trials at Villa Park for local youths to show what they could do as he searched for a new generation of players.

Birmingham, meanwhile, recruited former Derbyshire cricketer Harry Storer as their new manager, which proved a shrewd move. A strict disciplinarian who had studied tactics, he guided the club to the Football League (South) title and FA Cup semi-final as the professional game resumed at a low-key level in 1946, and two years later won promotion as Second Division champions.

There was conflict at Villa Park over the management of the team, with the board wanting more say in football affairs. When Massie resigned in protest in 1949, the club returned to their historic principle of picking the team by a committee of directors. They continued that way the following season, until in December – facing a huge battle to avoid relegation – they appointed George Martin as the new boss.

The former Luton and Newcastle manager was a bold thinker. He kept the club in the top flight, and among many changes was to convert Irishman Con Massie from centre-half to goalkeeper. But though he finished sixth in his first full season, when the next year brought mediocrity he was sacked and an old playing legend, Eric Houghton, was handed the job.

Houghton was loved by the Villa fans for his record scoring 170 goals in 390 games before the war, plus another 93 during wartime matches, and he won them over as a manager, too. Though he fought and won a relegation battle in 1956, the following season saw his team embark on a superb FA Cup run which ended by beating Manchester United 2-1 in the final. Villa fans loved that – and all the more because a year earlier the Blues had made it to Wembley but had controversially lost to Manchester City.

Birmingham's return to the top flight after the war had lasted only two seasons. Storer had surprisingly returned to former club Coventry a few months after winning promotion, and his replacement Bob Brocklebank bought good players such as Gordon Astall and Alex Govan, but never quite gelled them together.

They stayed in the Second Division until former player Arthur Turner took charge in November 1954 and galvanized the team into a run that brought promotion at his first attempt. Then came the best season of the club's history, finishing sixth in the First Division and that great FA Cup run.

The final became famous for Manchester City's German goalkeeper Bert Trautmann's bravery. He played on despite a collision with Birmingham's Joe Murphy, which it later emerged had dislocated five vertebrae in his neck. Another impact could have proved fatal. But Birmingham's players nursed their own grievance that Eddie Brown had scored twice in the first half, only for both to be disallowed for debatable offside decisions.

The Blues had become a pioneering club during this time. They installed floodlights at St Andrew's in 1956, two years before Villa caught on to the idea, and also experimented with European football – first with prestige friendlies under their lights and then in the newly created Inter Cities Fairs Cup.

Sadly, another attempt to innovate was to be less successful. In the middle of the 1957–58 season the board felt that manager Arthur Turner needed more support and appointed Pat Beasley to work with him as "joint manager". Turner learned of the decision only through the local press, and though there were smiles when the arrangement began, all was not well behind the scenes. Eight months later Turner walked out – and the decade ended with Birmingham only just surviving a relegation battle.

Record in the 1940s and '50s

Aston Villa:

Season	League	P	W	D	L	F	A	Pts	Position
1946–47	Div 1	42	18	9	15	67	53	45	8
1947–48	Div 1	42	19	9	14	65	57	47	6
1948–49	Div 1	42	16	10	16	60	76	42	10
1949–50	Div 1	42	15	12	15	61	61	42	12
1950–51	Div 1	42	12	13	17	66	68	37	15
1951–52	Div 1	42	19	9	14	79	70	47	6
1952–53	Div 1	42	14	13	15	63	61	41	11
1953–54	Div 1	42	16	9	17	70	68	41	13
1954–55	Div 1	42	20	7	15	72	73	47	6
1955–56	Div 1	42	11	13	18	52	69	35	20
1956–57	Div 1	42	14	15	13	65	55	43	10
1957–58	Div 1	42	16	7	19	73	86	39	14
1958–59	Div 1	42	20	6	16	84	68	46	9
1959–60	Div 2	42	25	9	8	89	43	59	1

FA Cup

1945–46	3-4, 1-1 v Derby County (sixth round, over two legs)
1946–47	1-5 v Burnley (third round)
1947–48	4-6 v Manchester United (third round)
1948–49	1-2 v Cardiff City (fourth round)

1949–50	2-2, 0-0, 0-3 v Middlesbrough (third round)	
1950–51	1-3 v Wolverhampton Wanderers (fourth round)	
1951–52	2-4 v Newcastle United (third round)	
1952–53	0-1 v Everton (sixth round)	
1953–54	1-5 v Arsenal (third round)	
1954–55	0-0, 2-2, 1-1, 0-0, 1-3 v Doncaster Rovers (fourth round)	
1955–56	1-4 v Arsenal (fourth round)	
1956–57	2-1 v Manchester United (final at Wembley Stadium)	
1957–58	1-1, 3-3, 0-2 v Stoke City (third round)	
1958–59	0-1 v Nottingham Forest (semi-final)	
1959–60	0-1 v Wolverhampton Wanderers (semi-final)	

Birmingham:

Season	League	P	W	D	L	F	A	Pts	Position
1946–47	Div 2	42	25	5	12	74	33	55	3
1947–48	Div 2	42	22	15	5	55	24	59	1
1948–49	Div 1	42	11	15	16	36	38	37	17
1949–50	Div 1	42	7	14	21	31	67	28	22
1950–51	Div 2	42	20	9	13	64	53	49	4
1951–52	Div 2	42	21	9	12	67	56	51	3
1952–53	Div 2	42	19	10	13	71	66	48	6
1953–54	Div 2	42	18	11	13	78	58	47	7
1954–55	Div 2	42	22	10	10	92	47	54	1
1955–56	Div 1	42	18	9	15	75	57	45	6
1956–57	Div 1	42	15	9	18	69	69	39	13
1957–58	Div 1	42	14	11	17	76	89	39	13
1958–59	Div 1	42	20	6	16	84	68	46	9
1959–60	Div 1	42	13	10	19	63	80	36	19

FA Cup

1945–46	1-1, 0-4 v Derby County (semi-final)	
1946–47	1-4 v Liverpool (sixth round)	
1947–48	0-2 v Notts County (third round)	

1948–49   1-1, 1-1, 1-2 v Leicester City (third round)

1949–50   0-3 v Swansea Town (third round)

1950–51   0-0, 1-2 v Blackpool (semi-final)

1951–52   0-1 v Leyton Orient (fourth round)

1952–53   1-1, 2-2, 0-1 v Tottenham Hotspur (sixth round)

1953–54   0-1 v Ipswich (fourth round)

1954–55   0-1 v Manchester City (sixth round)

1955–56   1-3 v Manchester City (final at Wembley Stadium)

1956–57   0-2 v Manchester United (semi-final)

1957–58   0-3 v York City (third round)

1958–59   1-1, 1-1, 0-5 v Nottingham Forest (fifth round)

1959–60   1-2 v Watford (third round)

European Competition

1956–58   Inter Cities Fairs Cup 4-3, 0-1, 1-2 v Barcelona (semi-final, two legs then replay in Basle)

1958–60   Inter Cities Fairs Cup 0-0, 1-4 v Barcelona (final, over two legs)

4th December 1948

Division One

Aston Villa 0

Birmingham 3

Stewart (2), Bodle

Attendance: 62,424

ASTON VILLA: *Rutherford, C. Martin, Cummings, A. Moss, F. Moss, E. Lowe, Mulraney, Dorsett, Ford, Edwards, L. Smith*

BIRMINGHAM: *Merrick, Green, Jennings, Harris, Duckhouse, Mitchell, Berry, Stewart, Dougall, Bodle, Roberts*

The task of rebuilding at the end of the Second World War was a challenge for every Football League side – and all the more so for Birmingham. Relegated just before hostilities began, they then suffered severe bomb damage to St Andrew's.

The task of lifting the club's fortunes fell to Harry Storer, who had managed nearby Coventry City for 14 years. A former England international who had also played county cricket for Derbyshire, he rose to the challenge and put together a side which lacked stars, but played with great organization.

They conceded just 24 goals in 42 League games winning promotion in 1948 and took that momentum into their return to the First Division, losing only one of the first dozen games.

It had come as a huge shock to the club then, when in November, despite having made a decent start to the campaign, Storer left to accept an offer to return to Highfield Road, and a replacement had still not been appointed by this time.

Just four players were on show from the previous meeting back in March of 1939 – Joe Rutherford and George Cummings of Villa plus Fred Harris and Dennis Jennings of the Blues.

So with some nine years having gone by since the teams last met in a First Division game, the anticipation of renewed rivalry between the two clubs meant a crowd of more than 60,000 crammed into Villa Park – but it was to be the Birmingham supporters who enjoyed the day most.

It took just 15 minutes for them to take the lead, a clever back-heel by Neil Dougall opening up a chance for Jackie Stewart to get his first goal since he had scored four against Manchester City at the start of September.

Villa began to get into the game but Blues centre-half Ted Duckhouse organized the defence superbly to make sure his team still led at half-time, although George Edwards did bring a good save out of Gil Merrick.

But with 66 minutes gone Stewart scored again – a free-kick by Harris was headed on by Harold Bodle and he got between two defenders to take an opportunistic chance.

Five minutes later Bodle put the game out of Villa's reach as he ran into position to meet Johnny Berry's centre and hooked it over Rutherford's head.

30th April 1949

Division One
Birmingham 0
Aston Villa 1
Craddock
Attendance: 45,120
BIRMINGHAM: *Merrick, McDonnell, Green, Dorman, Duckhouse, Ferris, Stewart, Jordan, Badham, Harris, Laing*
ASTON VILLA: *Rutherford, Parkes, Cummings, Powell, Martin, F. Moss, Edwards, Dorsett, Craddock, Dixon, Smith*

The task of replacing Harry Storer had been handed to a former Aston Villa player, Bob Brocklebank, who did a good job restoring some stability to St Andrew's as they adapted to life back in the First Division.

They remained well organized defensively, conceding only 38 goals in the campaign – the lowest of any side in the top flight that year. However, it was just as well because they scored only 38, failing to find the net in half of their matches.

So when Villa's reserve centre-forward Miller Craddock – called into action due to an injury to Trevor Ford – scored after six minutes in the away team's first attack, it was always going to be a tough afternoon for the Blues.

Martin McDonnell's mistake gave the ball to Leslie Smith, and the winger whipped in a cross that Craddock reached before Birmingham's defence could react.

Fred Harris wasted an immediate chance to equalize with a header that went wide, and in a fast but physical game he was unlucky to see a shot hit the bar just before half-time.

It was a bad-tempered match, with Craddock and Don Dorman

being spoken to by the referee after clashing with each other in the second half.

But Villa continued to dominate, with Con Martin in complete command in the centre of defence, and they were denied a second goal when Dickie Dorsett scored from a free-kick but the referee ordered it to be retaken.

10th December 1949

Division One

Aston Villa 1

Ford

Birmingham 1

Brennan

Attendance: 45,008

ASTON VILLA: *Rutherford, Parkes, Dorsett, Powell, Martin, F. Moss, Dixon, J. Harrison, Ford, Edwards, L. Smith*

BIRMINGHAM: *Merrick, Badham, Jennings, Boyd, Atkins, Dorman, Stewart, Jordan, Higgins, Brennan, Berry*

Alex Massie, who had managed Villa through the opening seasons after the war, caused a shock in the summer of 1949 by resigning from the post. He had been unhappy, feeling that the directors were trying to interfere in his team selection.

The club's response was to go back to their old and long-held tradition of having the directors pick the team, and they went all through this season without appointing a replacement.

It wasn't entirely successful, and with additional problems caused by injuries to goalkeeper Joe Rutherford and Leslie Smith, Villa had won only five of 19 games by the time they faced Birmingham in early December.

Heavy snow had fallen on the morning of the game, which the groundstaff worked hard to shovel away, but it left the pitch heavy and conditions difficult.

The game started quietly, with Blues centre-half Arthur Atkins paying close attention to Welsh international Trevor Ford who was Villa's danger man.

But with 35 minutes gone it was Ford who scored the opening goal, running on to a clever pass from James Harrison.

The lead lasted only five minutes, however. Rutherford was at fault, letting a shot from 25 yards out by Bobby Brennan slip through his grasp, and though he tried to claw it away, the referee Mr Evans ruled it had gone over the line.

Ford should have got a winner early in the second half, but was denied by Gil Merrick's excellent save at his feet.

29th April 1950

Division One
Birmingham 2
Trigg (2)
Aston Villa 2
Ford (2)
Attendance: 24,866
BIRMINGHAM: *Merrick, Green, Jennings, Boyd, Duckhouse, Ferris, Stewart, Brennan, Trigg, Harris, Berry*
ASTON VILLA: *Rutherford, Parkes, Dorsett, Powell, Martin, F. Moss, Dixon, Gibson, Ford, Goffin, L. Smith*

It was an emotional day for Birmingham skipper Fred Harris, playing his final game at St Andrew's after announcing his plans to retire following 17 years of service to the club.

A successful inside-forward in his early days, he had been converted during the war into a wing-half, before being made captain by Harry Storer and leading the side to promotion.

A brass band appeared on the pitch before kick-off, and played 'For he's a jolly good fellow' to mark the occasion, with the crowd singing in great heart.

The Blues tried to do the occasion justice once the game kicked off, and Joe Rutherford was the busier keeper even though it was Gil Merrick who made the most important save, diving at the feet of Trevor Ford.

Merrick had no luck, however, when the Welsh international put the visitors in front just before half-time. Leslie Smith beat two defenders before sending over a cross that picked out Ford, who mistimed his shot only to see it deceive Merrick and trickle just inside the post.

It was a significant blow for Birmingham who were fighting relegation, but news at half-time that rivals Charlton were losing at Derby encouraged them to fight back, and Bobby Brennan met a cross by Ray Ferris with a header that set up a chance for Cyril Trigg to score.

Trigg missed another golden chance, but did put Blues in front after 77 minutes, when Jackie Stewart's centre was deflected off a defender into his path and he struck a fierce shot that gave Joe Rutherford no chance.

But with rain teeming down, Merrick's handling let him down again as he dived at Smith's feet but the ball spun away and left Ford with an empty goal.

It was a cruel blow for Birmingham – and even worse as the game ended and they learned that Charlton had hit back to win at Derby to leave them bottom of the table and certain to be relegated with a game still to go.

5th September 1955

Division One

Aston Villa 0

Birmingham 0

Attendance: 56,935

ASTON VILLA: *Jones, Lynn, Aldis, Baxter, Martin, Crowe, Southren, Gibson, Hickson, Follan, McParland*

BIRMINGHAM: *Merrick, Hall, Green, Boyd, Newman, Warhurst, Astall, Kinsey, Brown, Murphy, Govan*

It took Birmingham five seasons to return to the First Division, the difference coming when Arthur Turner was appointed to replace Bob Brocklebank as manager half way through the 1954–55 season.

Promotion still came by the tiniest of margins, even though they won 15 of their last 22 matches. It took a 5-1 win at Doncaster on the final day of the season to clinch the Second Division Championship on goal average (the system used in those days long before goal difference was adopted in the 1976–77 season), with both Luton and Rotherham also boasting 54 points.

It meant the first derby of the season was eagerly awaited, but the outcome was a disappointment with neither team creating much in the way of chances.

Both sides seem to feel it was more important not to lose the encounter than to win it, and so the forwards on each team did an awful lot of work helping out their defenders and not enough trying to score goals for themselves.

Villa had a shade the better of the first half, and kept Gil Merrick reasonably busy but without ever really testing the England goalkeeper.

Manager Eric Houghton had struggled the previous season to find somebody to fill the club's number 9 jersey, and had tried to solve the problem by paying Everton £17,500 to sign Dave Hickson.

A man who had scored 63 goals in 139 games for the Toffees suffered a disappointing debut, however, with too many passes that went astray.

Not that Birmingham were much better. Their centre-forward Eddie Brown missed a good early chance, and while his pace occasionally troubled the home defence he was desperately out of form on the ball.

The second half became bad tempered. Peter McParland was

denied what looked a certain goal when he was tripped by full-back Jeff Hall as he broke free – what would nowadays merit a red card for a professional foul. The same thing happened to Brown when he was dashing goalwards and was fouled by Con Martin.

Near the end Merrick produced a superb double save that kept out McParland's header and then his follow-up shot, but neither side deserved to win.

21ˢᵗ September 1955

Division One

Birmingham 2

Brown, Astall

Aston Villa 2

Southren, Baxter

Attendance: 32,642

BIRMINGHAM: *Merrick, Hall, Badham, Boyd, Smith, Warhurst, Astall, Kinsey, Brown, Murphy, Govan*

ASTON VILLA: *Jones, Lynn, Aldis, Baxter, Martin, Crowe, Southren, Dixon, Hickson, A. Moss, McParland*

In the two weeks between the bad-tempered Villa Park fixture and the return at St Andrew's there had been much debate about the poor sportsmanship on show.

As a result both teams endeavoured to bring a different attitude to the game, and the result was a match that was every bit as thrilling as the first encounter had been tedious and tetchy.

If neither team deserved to win the first match, then neither deserved to lose the second. It was a bright and entertaining game of four goals, much fast and sporting play, with none of the petty fouls which had scarred the previous meeting.

Birmingham set the tone with their first goal after 23 minutes, with the ball moving up the left from Jack Badham to Peter Murphy, and then to winger Alex Govan. When he put over a hard, swinging centre it was met by Eddie Brown with a brilliant header, half twisting as he jumped to direct the ball beyond the reach of goalkeeper Keith Jones.

It was, according to the *Birmingham Post* report, "a brilliant goal which so delighted the centre-forward after his astonishing run of misses recently that he gave a second leap in the air and danced his way through congratulating colleagues back to the centre spot".

There was an element of luck about Villa's equalizer. A shot from Tommy Southren beat Gil Merrick's dive but hit the post, only for the ball to rebound against the goalkeeper's fallen body and ricochet back into the net.

The pace picked up further after the interval with Villa doing most of the pressing, but it was Birmingham who regained the lead after 67 minutes.

Villa failed to deal with a good cross from the right, and the ball dropped to Gordon Astall on the edge of the area from where he struck a superb first-time volley that gave Jones no chance.

But within three minutes the game was level again, Southren moving out wide to launch an attack that ended with Bill Baxter sweeping his low cross into the goal.

The only disappointment for Villa was that centre-forward Hickson again failed to score. He ended up playing only a dozen games for the club and getting just one goal before moving on to Huddersfield.

27th October 1956

Division One

Aston Villa 3

Lynn, Roberts, Sewell

Birmingham 1

Astall

Attendance: **54,927**

ASTON VILLA: *Sims, Lynn, Aldis, Baxter, Dugdale, Saward, L. Smith, Sewell, Dixon, Roberts, McParland*

BIRMINGHAM: *Merrick, Hall, Badham, Watts, Smith, Warhurst, Astall, Orritt, Brown, Murphy, Govan*

Beaten FA Cup finalists the previous season, Birmingham had lost only three times in their first 13 games and had started the season in sensational style with winger Alex Govan scoring three hat-tricks in nine days to earn wins over Portsmouth, Newcastle and Preston.

But any optimism that Arthur Turner's team might have felt arriving at Villa Park disappeared within two minutes as Villa took the lead with a well-worked corner routine.

While both attackers and defenders packed the penalty area waiting for a cross, Les Smith rolled the ball back to where full-back Stan Lynn came charging forward and struck the ball from 15 yards beyond the grasp of Gil Merrick.

After seizing the initiative Villa continued to attack, with centre-forward Johnny Dixon combining well alongside youngster Ken Roberts.

Roberts, 20, had set a Football League record when he made his debut for Wrexham at the age of just 15 years and 158 days, but had struggled after moving to Villa and had been made available for transfer the previous summer.

But he grabbed a chance to impress, and scored a terrific goal to put his team two ahead after 25 minutes, picking up the ball on the edge of the penalty area and slamming home a ferocious shot.

Shortly after that, Villa were effectively reduced to 10 men when Bill Baxter collected a knee injury, and had to spend the rest of the game limping on the left wing.

But it made little difference to the overall pattern in what was the home team's best performance of that season so far.

In fact it was just before half-time that the third goal came, with Roberts again involved as he found some space and supplied a perfect pass for Jackie Sewell to score.

The Blues at least improved after the interval, but their forwards struggled to take any pressure away from the defenders.

And in the descending fog it did little to lift their gloom even when with seven minutes left Gordon Astall finished off a good left-wing move to get a goal that was little consolation for a poor display.

10th April 1957

Division One

Birmingham 1

Murphy

Aston Villa 2

Chapman (2)

Attendance: 29,853

BIRMINGHAM: *Merrick, Hall, Green, Larkin, T. Smith, Warhurst, Neale, Kinsey, Brown, Murphy, Govan*

ASTON VILLA: *Sims, Jackson, Aldis, Crowther, Dugdale, Birch, L. Smith, Chapman, Pace, Dixon, Southren*

How times changed. A year earlier Birmingham had been all ready to go to Wembley while Villa were struggling to keep their place in the First Division. Now it was Villa who were on their way to an FA Cup final appearance and victory while the Blues were fading – and had not won a home match since the turn of the year.

Just to emphasize the change, Villa arrived at St Andrew's with a side that was suffering from the effects of their Cup run. Replays against both Burnley and West Bromwich Albion meant this was their 12th game in 39 days and the outcome of that was a side weakened by four injuries as well as the fact that Peter McParland was away on international duty.

The fates smiled kindly on Eric Houghton's side, however, as a rare goalkeeping blunder by Gil Merrick presented the visitors with the opening goal after just nine minutes.

Merrick, who had by now lost his place as England keeper, somehow allowed a harmless-looking 20-yard shot from Roy Chapman to slip through his hands and drop behind him into the net.

A Blues side who were already lacking in confidence visibly slumped further, and Villa took command in the 21st minute.

Birmingham's centre-half Trevor Smith had got away with a bad mistake that had presented Johnny Dixon with an easy chance, only for the inside-right to put the ball wide. But another error was more costly, as he allowed Les Smith far too much room and the winger's cross gave Roy Chapman the easiest of chances.

City at least pulled themselves back into the game before the interval – a corner from Alex Govan finding Peter Murphy unmarked.

They might even have equalized after the break, as first a shot from Eddie Brown hit the post and then Murphy was denied by a brave save at his feet.

The second half became an increasingly physical battle, but Villa held on to complete their victory.

24th August 1957

Division One
Birmingham 3
Brown, Kinsey, Murphy
Aston Villa 1
McParland
Attendance: **50,780**
BIRMINGHAM: *Schofield, Hall, Green, Watts, Smith, Neal, Astall, Kinsey, Brown, Murphy, Govan*
ASTON VILLA: *Sims, Lynn, Aldis, Crowther, Dugdale, Saward, Smith, Sewell, Myerscough, Dixon, McParland*

Fresh from the triumph of lifting the FA Cup at Wembley, Villa began a new season full of optimism for what lay ahead.

And if they couldn't kick off with a home fixture, what better place to start than on the ground of their fiercest rivals at St Andrew's?

The attraction brought a huge crowd, with many still trying to get in at kick-off time. A desperate Tannoy announcement was put out to encourage those already in the ground to squeeze forward to make more room.

Peter McParland, the two-goal hero of the Wembley win, began in impressive style hitting the side-netting with a fierce shot after only a few seconds of the game had passed.

But then Birmingham produced a flowing move to take the lead in the ninth minute. Alex Govan swung a cross to the right where Gordon Astall outjumped two defenders to head it back into the path of Eddie Brown, who set up the chance for Noel Kinsey.

Villa drew level in the 24th minute thanks to McParland. Stan Lynn took a free-kick 10 yards outside the penalty area, Leslie Smith collected the ball and crossed it back into the box where McParland met it with a spectacular diving header from 10 yards out.

Johnny Dixon went close shortly afterwards, juggling the ball past three City defenders but lobbing the ball just wide.

And the FA Cup holders were punished for the miss when in the 40th minute they failed to clear Astall's corner and it was volleyed back with so much power by Peter Murphy that goalkeeper Nigel Sims had no time to react before the ball had flown past him.

The Blues were without their stalwart goalkeeper Gil Merrick, who was missing the opening game of the season for the first time in his 12 seasons with the club, but his deputy Johnny Schofield proved a capable stand-in.

He saved from Billy Myerscough after good work by Dixon, and then again from Jackie Sewell, and deserved his luck when full-back Stan Lynn burst forward but hit the underside of the bar. The ball bounced down on the line, and the Villa players appealed for a goal but referee Mr Clough ignored their claims.

Villa had more cause to curse the referee with 71 minutes gone. Sims came to collect a cross from Noel Kinsey but was impeded by two forwards and dropped the ball for Brown to put it into the empty net.

Villa appealed in vain for a foul, and Birmingham had little trouble seeing out the rest of the match to secure their first win against Villa in a First Division game at St Andrew's since 1938.

21st December 1957

Division One
Aston Villa 0
Birmingham 2
Brown, Kinsey
Attendance: 41,118
ASTON VILLA: *Sims, Lynn, Aldis, Crowe, Dugdale, Saward, Smith, Crowther, Hitchens, Dixon, McParland*
BIRMINGHAM: *Merrick, Hall, Farmer, Larkin, Smith, Neal, Hooper, Kinsey, Brown, Murphy, Astall*

This was a historic game – and not only because it marked the first time in more than 50 years that the Blues had completed a League double over their old enemy.

Gerry Hitchens, who would go on to score an astonishing 96 goals in his 160 appearances for Villa, was making his debut after a £22,500 transfer from Cardiff.

It was big news. Hitchens, who began his working life as a miner, had started his professional career playing for Coventry and turned down a trial at West Bromwich Albion because he didn't think he would be good enough.

Cardiff had signed him for just £1,500 and turned a handsome profit on a player who would four years later play for England and then move to Italy with Inter Milan.

On this day, however, Hitchens showed plenty of promise but couldn't find a goal as his reward. The *Birmingham Sports Argus* report described him as having "a deceptively casual air, but he can put defenders in a tizzy by holding the ball. He can beat a man – ask Trevor Smith, Bunny Larkin and Jeff Hall. And he has a cracking shot in that right foot."

All that came to nothing, however, as goals from Eddie Brown and Noel Kinsey put Birmingham fans in the party mood ahead of Christmas.

The real turning point, however, was when Gil Merrick saved a penalty in the 69th minute. Full-back Stan Lynn lashed the ball with awesome power, but the former England keeper somehow managed to get to it as the ball went fast to his left.

At that point the Blues were already leading through Brown's header from a Harry Hooper cross, but had come under pressure and been fortunate when Stan Crowther hit the post.

But Merrick's save changed the momentum, and Kinsey was the hero as he got onto the end of a left-wing cross with a perfectly timed header.

23rd August 1958

Division One

Aston Villa 1

Lynn (pen)

Birmingham 1

Murphy

Attendance: 55,198

ASTON VILLA: *Sims, Lynn, Aldis, Birch, Dugdale, Saward, Southren, Hitchens, Dixon, Myerscough, McParland*

BIRMINGHAM: *Merrick, Hall, Green, Larkin, Smith, Neal, Hooper, Orritt, Brown, Murphy, Taylor*

Birmingham had begun an experiment at the end of the previous season with Pat Beasley handed the title of joint manager alongside Arthur Turner.

It was clear there were tensions between them, however, despite a late run of results that had seen them finish well clear of the relegation zone and a place above Villa on goal average.

But as a new season kicked off the Blues had troubles behind the scenes which would ultimately lead to Turner, the man who had taken the club to an FA Cup final two years earlier and been responsible for one of the best periods of St Andrew's history, walking out at the start of September.

None of this was widely known on the opening day of the new campaign with sunshine bathing Villa Park and a huge crowd packed in to see what was in store.

Blues had 21-year-old winger Brian Taylor, signed from Walsall during the summer, making his debut while veteran Johnny Dixon was attempting a comeback for Villa after missing most of the previous campaign through injury.

It was a scrappy and unsatisfactory game, however. Birmingham were just about the best side in the first half, with Harry Hooper the best forward on show.

It was Hooper's thoughtful work that set up the chance from which Peter Murphy headed them into the lead after 14 minutes. Villa fought back from that, but there was little composure about their work and Gil Merrick was barely tested although Gerry Hitchens had a chance just before the break but shot wide.

Dixon produced a splendid 25-yard shot after the interval which Merrick turned away, and that spurred Villa into a spell of pressure which ended with the equalizer.

Billy Myerscough's cross hit the outstretched arm of Bunny Larkin, and although the Blues defender angrily claimed it was accidental, referee Mr Bond from London pointed to the spot.

It was a big moment for Stan Lynn whose penalty had been saved by Merrick in the last encounter, but the full-back kept his nerve and drove the spot-kick firmly home.

Myerscough and McParland both missed chances but with the youthful Taylor's energy starting to make life tough for the experienced Lynn in the closing minutes, Villa ended up being glad to take one point – especially when Lynn had to head Hooper's effort away from under the bar in injury time.

20th December 1958

Division One

Birmingham 4

Astall (pen), Jackson (2), Neal

Aston Villa 1

Hazelden

Attendance: 31,857

BIRMINGHAM: *Merrick, Hall, Allen, Watts, Smith, Neal, Astall, Gordon, Jackson, Larkin, Taylor*

ASTON VILLA: *Sims, Lynn, Aldis, Dixon, Dugdale, Crowe, Smith, Sewell, Myerscough, Hazelden, McParland*

If the opening day of the season had not been good for Villa, by the time December came they were a club in crisis.

Eric Houghton had left his position as manager in the middle of November a few days after a 6-3 defeat at Leicester in a game in which his team had been 3-1 up at half-time.

More than a month later no replacement had been appointed, and the club had slid to the bottom of the table.

A circular issued to shareholders said: "The need of a successor is more than apparent and we can only hope that a choice will soon be made, not necessarily from the list of applicants but perhaps by an honourable invitation to an already successful man, giving him a fitting salary, a comparatively free hand and suitable contract in which to show his worth."

That policy would eventually lead to Joe Mercer's appointment on Christmas Eve, a decision hastened by the miserable performance in this match in which Birmingham were always the better side.

Conditions could not have been tougher with steady rain falling. The pitch, bad at the start with puddles and mud, rapidly became appalling.

As a result Villa decided not to risk Ron Wylie who had an injury, and Walter Hazelden came in at inside-left.

The impact the conditions might have became clear within a minute when a backpass by Trevor Smith did not reach Gil Merrick, and he had to rush from goal to grab the ball before Johnny Dixon could reach it.

The Blues adapted to the conditions better, driving the ball forward so as not to risk it getting stuck in the puddles – but it was another bad backpass that gave Villa the lead. This time Hazelden was quicker than Merrick to get to the loose ball and apply the finishing touch.

The youngster was unlucky not to get a second when he hit the post after the interval, but then the game swung as Bunny Larkin was brought down by Jimmy Dugdale and Gordon Astall scored from the resulting penalty.

Astall began the move from which Alex Jackson put the Blues in front shortly after, and from there the floodgates opened.

Jackson punished goalkeeper Nigel Sims for a handling error in the 77th minute, and with three minutes left Dick Neal completed a thumping win which left Villa stranded at the foot of the table while they got four points clear.

It proved to be a crucial moment. Mercer's appointment a few days later brought about a brief revival in Villa's season, and they raised hopes by getting to the semi-final of the FA Cup.

But a horrid spell of nine games without a win at the end of the season left them with too much to do, and relegation was confirmed when they drew 1-1 at West Bromwich Albion on the final day.

Chapter Six

The 1960s

It might have been the Swinging Sixties in Carnaby Street, but if there was a song from the Flower Power era that suited Aston Villa, it would have been the Rolling Stones' "Nineteenth Nervous Breakdown".

The decade began with so much promise as Joe Mercer – unable to halt a slide towards relegation when he was appointed in December 1958 – put together an exciting young side who earned the nickname of the "Mercer Minors".

He introduced youngsters like Alan Deakin, John Sleeuwenhoek, Alan Baker and Charlie Aitken, who would go on to become the club's record appearance holder. And the fearless enthusiasm they showed captured the imagination of the Villa fans as they stormed back to the top flight in 1960 as Second Division champions and also reached the FA Cup semi-finals.

They won the inaugural Football League Cup in 1961, finishing ninth in the First Division, and the following season moved up to seventh with an appearance in the FA Cup quarter-finals.

Across town Birmingham had begun the decade with just as much optimism, relishing their adventures in Europe as they twice reached the final of the Inter Cities Fairs Cup, losing the first to Barcelona and then in a controversial clash to Roma. Manager Gil Merrick, a playing legend as the goalkeeper of the 1930s FA Cup final team who had also won 25 England caps, also landed their first major trophy – all the more sweet as they beat Villa in the two-legged League Cup final.

That clash proved a peak for both teams. A year later Blues had to battle for survival, beating Sheffield United 3-0 on the final day of the season to avoid relegation, and Merrick was sacked. Bitter at his treatment, it was years before he would set foot inside St Andrew's again. His successor Joe Mallett's reign proved disastrous, as the Blues finished bottom in 1965 and were back in the Second Division.

Birmingham's answer was to persuade Stan Cullis, the manager who had inspired Wolves through their glory days of the 1950s, to come out of retirement – but despite breaking the club's transfer record to buy Barry Bridges for £55,000, the nearest he came to a return to the First Division was finishing fourth in 1968, still six points outside the promotion places.

If Birmingham had their problems, however, at Villa Park things were even worse. Joe Mercer felt the pressure of failing to deliver success in the First Division and resigned through ill health in 1964. His successor Dick Taylor spent a hapless three years in charge which ended with relegation.

His replacement was Tommy Cummings, who had made his name as a centre-half for Burnley and was considered a bright managerial prospect after success with Mansfield Town. But he was totally out of his depth at Villa. Average attendances slipped to below 20,000 as the team finished 16th in Division Two, and when the following season began with just two wins in 18 League matches, he was sacked.

There was upheaval in the boardroom. Doug Ellis had just been installed as the new chairman, and appointed Tommy Docherty as manager. The colourful former Chelsea boss produced a dramatic run of results to stave off relegation, and the next season began with a huge wave of optimism and big spending on new players. For whatever reason, though, they didn't gel, and Docherty was sacked a few days after the end of the 1960s with the club rooted to the foot of Division Two and destined to end up in the third tier for the first time in their history.

Record in the 1960s

Aston Villa:

Season	League	P	W	D	L	F	A	Pts	Position
1960–61	Div 1	42	17	9	16	78	77	43	9
1961–62	Div 1	42	18	8	16	65	56	44	7
1962–63	Div 1	42	15	8	19	62	68	38	15
1963–64	Div 1	42	11	12	19	62	71	34	19
1964–65	Div 1	42	16	5	21	57	82	37	16
1965–66	Div 1	42	15	6	21	69	80	36	16
1966–67	Div 1	42	11	7	24	54	85	29	21
1967–68	Div 2	42	15	7	20	54	64	37	16
1968–69	Div 2	42	12	14	16	37	48	38	18
1969–70	Div 2	42	8	13	21	36	62	29	21

FA Cup

1960–61	0-2 v Tottenham Hotspur (fifth round)
1961–62	0-2 v Tottenham Hotspur (sixth round)
1962–63	0-1 v Manchester United (fourth round)
1963–64	0-0, 1-2 v Aldershot (third round)
1964–65	1-1, 0-0, 1-3 v Wolverhampton Wanderers (fifth round)
1965–66	1-2 v Leicester City (third round)
1966–67	0-1 v Liverpool (fourth round)
1967–68	0-1 v Rotherham United (fourth round)
1968–69	2-3 v Tottenham Hotspur (fifth round)
1969–70	1-1, 0-1 v Charlton Athletic (third round)

Football League Cup

1960–61	0-2, 3-0 v Rotherham United (final, over two legs)
1961–62	2-3 v Ipswich Town (third round)
1962–63	1-3, 0-0 v Birmingham (final over two legs)
1963–64	0-2 v West Ham United (third round)
1964–65	2-3, 1-1 v Chelsea (semi-final over two legs)

1965–66	1-3 v West Bromwich Albion (fifth round)
1966–67	1-6 v West Bromwich Albion (second round)
1967–68	1-3 v Northampton Town (second round)
1968–69	1-4 v Tottenham Hotspur (second round)
1969–70	1-2 v West Bromwich Albion (second round)

Birmingham:

Season	League	P	W	D	L	F	A	Pts	Position
1960–61	Div 1	42	14	6	22	62	84	34	19
1961–62	Div 1	42	14	10	18	65	81	38	17
1962–63	Div 1	42	10	13	19	63	90	33	20
1963–64	Div 1	42	11	7	24	54	92	29	20
1964–65	Div 1	42	8	11	23	64	96	27	22
1965–66	Div 2	42	16	9	17	70	75	41	10
1966–67	Div 2	42	16	8	18	70	66	40	10
1967–68	Div 2	42	19	14	9	83	51	52	4
1968–69	Div 2	42	18	8	16	73	59	44	7
1969–70	Div 2	42	11	11	20	51	78	33	18

FA Cup

1960–61	1-1, 1-2 v Leicester City (fifth round)
1961–62	3-3, 2-4 v Tottenham Hotspur (third round)
1962–63	3-3, 0-2 v Bury (third round)
1963–64	1-2 v Port Vale (third round)
1964–65	2-4 v West Ham (third round)
1965–66	1-2 v Leicester City (fourth round)
1966–67	0-0, 0-6 v Tottenham Hotspur (sixth round)
1967–68	0-2 v West Bromwich Albion (semi-final)
1968–69	2-2, 2-6 v Manchester United (fifth round)
1969–70	0-3 v Chelsea (third round)

Football League Cup

| 1960–61 | 0-0, 1-3 v Plymouth (third round) |

1961–62   1-1, 0-2 v Swindon (first round)

1962–63   3-1, 0-0 v Aston Villa (final, over two legs)

1963–64   0-2 v Norwich (second round)

1964–65   0-3 v Chelsea (second round)

1965–66   1-2 v Mansfield (second round)

1966–67   1-4, 1-3 v Queens Park Rangers (semi-final, over two legs)

1967–68   1-3 v Derby County (third round)

1968–69   0-1 v Chelsea (second round)

1969–70   0-2 v Brighton (second round)

European Competition

1960–61   Inter Cities Fairs Cup 2-2, 0-2 v AS Roma (final, over
           two legs)

1961–62   Inter Cities Fairs Cup 2-5, 1-0 v RCD Espanyol
           (second round)

22nd October 1960

Division One

Aston Villa 6

O'Neill (2), Hitchens (3), McParland

Birmingham 2

Hellawell, Thomson (og)

Attendance: 44,722

ASTON VILLA: *Sims, Neal, Winton, Thomson, Dugdale, Seward,
MacEwan, O'Neill, Hitchens, Wylie, McParland*

BIRMINGHAM: *Schofield, Farmer, Allen, Watts, Sissons, Neal, Hellawell,
Rudd, Gordon, Singer, Astall*

There can have been few more dramatic derby debuts than the one
made by Alan O'Neill, signed a few days earlier from Sunderland for
a £10,000 fee.

The inside-right marked his opening appearance in claret and
blue by scoring with his first touch of the ball and went on to get

another goal as a Gerry Hitchens hat-trick helped towards the most comprehensive win in the fixture for 65 years.

The 23-year-old's strike came after just 20 seconds, hitting a left-foot shot from Peter McParland's cross that gave Johnny Schofield no chance.

Minutes later the Blues goalkeeper was thankful not to be picking the ball out of his net again as Ron Wylie's effort struck the bar.

It wasn't all one-way traffic, however, with Gordon Astall missing a good chance as the Blues began to dominate the game – only for Villa to get a second against the run of play. Wylie made the opening this time, with an incisive pass to where Hitchens beat centre-half Graham Sissons before finishing calmly.

Birmingham blew a big chance to get back into the game, when with 34 minutes gone Bobby Thomson fouled Jimmy Singer, but Astall's penalty kick was brilliantly saved by Nigel Sims.

McParland scored a great individual goal just after half-time, and two tight offside decisions denied them further goals.

Even when Mike Hellawell pulled a goal back for the Blues with a header, it took Villa less than a minute to restore their advantage as O'Neill began and ended a superb move involving McParland.

In pouring rain Villa took firm control, and Hitchens completed his hat-trick with goals in the last six minutes – the Blues having the consolation only of an own goal by Thomson.

Schofield couldn't be blamed for the margin of the defeat – his defenders let him down badly as the home team took over.

11th March 1961

Division One
Birmingham 1
Singer
Aston Villa 1
Hitchens
Attendance: 41,656

BIRMINGHAM: *Withers, Farmer, Sissons, Watts, Smith, Neal, Astall, Bloomfield, Harris, Singer, Taylor*
ASTON VILLA: *Sidebottom, Neal, Lee, Crowe, Dugdale, Deakin, MacEwan, Thomson, Hitchens, Wylie, McParland*

After returning to the First Division under the management of Joe Mercer, Villa had made a decent start to the campaign, but from Christmas onwards they began to have trouble – and they arrived at St Andrew's without a single League win since the turn of the year.

Maybe it was a result of a frantic Cup fixture list. Mercer's side were on their way to winning the newly created League Cup, and had also fought their way through FA Cup replays against Bristol Rovers and Peterborough before getting knocked out by Spurs.

Either way they thought they were finally on their way to a victory when Gerry Hitchens, hat-trick hero of the Villa Park rout back in October, gave them the lead after just seven minutes.

Gordon Lee, a 25-year-old utility player, was brought in by Mercer at the expense of Jock Winton for his first appearance after more than two years of reserve football – and he justified the decision with a raking pass that sent Hitchens into space for his 24th goal of the campaign.

The Blues attempted to fight back, and in a niggling game Ron Wylie had his name taken just before the break when he kicked the ball away after City had been awarded a free-kick.

But in truth Birmingham failed to create too many chances, and they had to rely on defenders Trevor Smith and Dick Neal to keep them in the game, with Brian Farmer also giving a stout display.

That eventually reaped its reward as their team began to gain more possession, and four minutes from time a period of intense pressure ended with Jimmy Singer grabbing an equalizer, finding space to meet a cross from Jimmy Harris.

It was heartbreaking for Villa who thought they had finally come up with a victory – and all the more so when Hitchens got the ball in the net a minute later only for the referee Mr Kelly to rule it out for a marginal offside decision.

28th October 1961

Division One

Aston Villa 1

McParland

Birmingham 3

Harris (2), Orritt

Attendance: **49,532**

ASTON VILLA: *Sidebottom, Neal, Aitken, Crowe, Sleeuwenhoek, Deakin, Ashe, Tindall, McParland, Wylie, Burrows*

BIRMINGHAM: *Schofield, Lynn, Sissons, Hennessey, Smith, Beard, Hellawell, Bloomfield, Harris, Orritt, Auld*

As another huge crowd packed into Villa Park nobody wanted to be late, with memories of the 20-second goal by Alan O'Neill which had got the game off to a firecracker of a start a year earlier.

This one began in equally dramatic style – except this time it was the Blues who led inside the opening minute.

The goal came from a peach of a four-man move started by Bryan Orritt, taken on by Terry Hennessey and Mike Hellawell before Jimmy Harris supplied the finish with just 39 seconds played.

Peter McParland missed an open goal for the chance to equalize after 26 minutes, but it was a sign of how much pressure Villa were under that the centre-forward immediately won applause by chasing 30 yards to break up a Birmingham attack.

Not long afterwards goalkeeper Johnny Schofield sighed with relief as he was caught off his line by a long shot from Harry Burrows, but the ball dropped just over the bar.

Just before half-time Birmingham increased their lead. Villa were waiting for an offside flag that didn't come as Orritt went through to receive Jimmy Bloomfield's pass, and he ran on to finish from close range.

McParland raised hopes when he got a goal back in the 50th minute with a thundering header from a centre by Norman Ashe.

But they were soon dashed again, Harris converting with a header after Hennessey's excellent pass had sent Orritt racing clear to put in an accurate cross.

The visitors went on to clinch their fourth win in five games – they could have had another goal but in the final minute an effort by Hellawell was controversially ruled offside.

17th March 1962

Division One
Birmingham 0
Aston Villa 2
Burrows, Wylie
Attendance: 43,489
BIRMINGHAM: *Schofield, Lynn, Sissons, Hennessey, Smith, Beard, Hellawell, Bloomfield, Harris, Leek, Auld*
ASTON VILLA: *Sims, Briggs, Neal, Crowe, Dugdale, Deakin, Ewing, Baker, Thomson, Wylie, Burrows*

Manager Joe Mercer was attempting to bring through more of Villa's young players and they were getting a growing reputation – dubbed the "Mercer Minors" or the "Mini Mercers" by the local and national press.

On this occasion he certainly needed the resources of a large pool of promising reserve players as injuries forced him to make six changes for the derby. That included giving a debut to 19-year-old right-back Wilson Briggs, who partnered John Neal in the absence of both Gordon Lee and Charlie Aitken.

Briggs made two excellent early interceptions to build his confidence, and from there Birmingham's comparatively expensive forward line had little joy against the bargain-priced defence of the visiting team.

In fact by the end the *Sports Argus* was posing a question over what Mercer would do when he next selected a team, as none of the youngsters he had chosen deserved to be left out when their more experienced team-mates returned.

Villa moved the ball smartly in attack, and deserved to be in the lead after just 14 minutes through their top-scorer Harry Burrows.

Ron Wylie's pass opened up a gap and the left-winger made no mistake as he ran on to the ball and slipped it beyond the reach of the advancing Johnny Schofield.

Villa had the ball in the net again three minutes later, but referee Mr Leuty ruled that Bobby Thomson had fouled the goalkeeper in the process of scoring.

It was a bad-tempered match. Aston Villa's Tommy Ewing and Neal both required lengthy treatment after being on the wrong end of fierce tackles, while Mr Leuty lectured both Burrows and Mike Hellawell after a flare-up between the two men.

Villa's second goal came in the 36th minute, with right-winger Ewing starting a flowing move that ended with Alan Baker drawing two defenders, before squaring a pass from which Ron Wylie couldn't miss.

Both sides finished the game with 10 men after Jimmy Dugdale and Bertie Auld were carried off in the 69th minute with head injuries following a goalmouth clash.

27th October 1962

Division One
Birmingham 3
Lynn (pen), Leek (2)
Aston Villa 2
O'Neill, Burrows (pen)
Attendance: 42,228
BIRMINGHAM: *Withers, Lynn, Sissons, Watts, Smith, Hennessey, Hellawell, Stubbs, Harris, Leek, Auld*

ASTON VILLA: *Sidebottom, Lee, Aitken, Crowe, Sleeuwenhoek, Deakin, Ewing, O'Neill, Thomson, Wylie, Burrows*

Birmingham manager Gil Merrick was absent from this game, away on a secret scouting mission in his efforts to strengthen a side that had made a faltering start to the season.

Their win over Wolves the week before was only the third of the campaign, and Merrick was anxious to reinforce an attack that had failed to score in eight of 14 previous League matches.

In the event he missed an absolute cracker of a game in which his side came out on top from arguably the most dramatic 18 minutes of any of the derby matches which had gone before.

There was little sign of the drama to come after a quiet first half in which Birmingham's Scottish winger Bertie Auld had been the most prominent player.

Auld, who had just asked to come off the transfer list, turned in a display of great danger and Villa right-back Gordon Lee endured a tough time trying to keep him quiet.

The game burst into life after 55 minutes, however, when Alan O'Neill – who himself had refused a transfer to Plymouth earlier in the week – completed a glorious passing move from deep in Villa's half with a well-taken goal.

But almost immediately Auld was brought down by John Sleeuwenhoek. Villa fans knew all about the penalty-taking prowess of full-back Stan Lynn – he had scored in derbies for them. The trouble was that he had been transferred to the Blues and this time his old club were on the receiving end as he slammed the ball home with block-busting power.

Within seconds of the restart there was controversy as referee Mr Tirebuck ruled that Trevor Smith had fouled Bobby Thomson and Harry Burrows showed he could smash a spot-kick every bit as hard as his old team-mate.

The Halifax-based referee was immediately in the middle of

another row. Villa goalkeeper Geoff Sidebottom was knocked out in a collision as Ken Leek met Auld's free-kick to score with a header, but the goal stood.

Leek was the hero again with the winner in the 73rd minute, slamming home a fearsome shot from the edge of the area.

16th March 1963

Division One

Aston Villa 4

Woosnam, Deakin, Baker, Burrows (pen)

Birmingham 0

Attendance: 40,400

ASTON VILLA: *Sidebottom, Fraser, Aitken, Crowe, Sleeuwenhoek, Deakin, Ewing, Baker, Thomson, Woosnam, Burrows*

BIRMINGHAM: *Schofield, Lynn, Green, Hennessey, Smith, Beard, Hellawell, Stubbs, Harris, Leek, Auld*

Joe Mercer's big mid-season transfer move was to sign Phil Woosnam from West Ham for £27,500 at the start of December.

Mercer, worried at the lack of goals from his team, believed the experienced Welsh international could solve the problem for him – but it was a move that didn't immediately work out.

At the age of 30 he was just beginning to go past the peak of his powers, and although he did ultimately score 23 goals in 106 League games, his first campaign brought only two in 18.

This was one of his good days, however. He not only opened the scoring for Villa after 23 minutes but was the architect of a resounding victory, leading the line with power, speed and guile.

He supplied the passes for two of the four goals for what was agreed to be the best of his seven games since his transfer – and with the able support of Alan Baker and Harry Burrows, the Blues were always second-best.

Birmingham were going through a difficult few weeks. Beaten

4-3 at Wolves seven days earlier, they were without Jimmy Bloomfield who had been placed on the transfer list.

Even Stan Lynn, given a chance to score from the penalty spot as he had done in the derby earlier in the season, saw his effort brilliantly saved by Geoff Sidebottom.

Villa's dominance in the first half was total and they were three up by half-time. Woosnam's goal came after the visitors failed to clear a corner. Four minutes later the Welshman played a superb diagonal pass that sent Alan Deakin clear and he ran fully 30 yards without being challenged before scoring.

Alan Baker got on the end of a Tommy Ewing cross to make it three, and with Birmingham's morale broken by Lynn's failure to put away his penalty, the result was a formality. Burrows wrapped it up in the second half with a spot-kick of his own.

23rd May 1963

Football League Cup Final
First Leg
Birmingham 3
Leek (2), Bloomfield
Aston Villa 1
Thomson
Attendance: 31,902
BIRMINGHAM: *Schofield, Lynn, Green, Hennessey, Smith, Beard, Hellawell, Bloomfield, Harris, Leek, Auld*
ASTON VILLA: *Sims, Fraser, Aitken, Crowe, Sleeuwenhoek, Lee, Baker, Graham, Thomson, Wylie, Burrows*

It had been a strange season for both clubs – not least because of the hardest winter of the century which had brought snow from Boxing Day right through to March.

Villa had played a couple of games during that period but the Blues went from 22nd December to 2nd March without a single

ABOVE: Birmingham's first home at Muntz Street – some 20,000 supporters squeezed in to see their opening First Division game against Aston Villa in September 1894.

LEFT: Frank Womack set a club record 491 League appearances for Birmingham between 1908 and 1928.

RIGHT: Aston Villa captain Andy Ducat before the start of the 1920 FA Cup final.

LEFT: Tom "Pongo" Waring was Aston Villa's big goalscoring star of the 1930s.

BELOW: Aston Villa centre-forward Billy Walker shakes hands with Prince Henry before the 1920 FA Cup final. Walker made 22 appearances in the second city derby.

RIGHT: Bradford (right) with Johnny Crosbie and Stan Davies on a training run during the 1928 season. Bradford was a constant menace to Villa and scored eight goals in his 23 derby games.

LEFT: Jimmy McMullan, Aston Villa's first manager in the 1930s. His reign was far from a success.

BELOW: Birmingham's team in the 1938–39 season. They won 3-0 at home to Villa but lost 5-1 in March on the way to getting relegated.
Back row, left to right: Dennis Jennings, Walter Halsall, Frank Clack, Ernie Sykes, Jack Shaw, Owen Madden, Jackie Brown, W. Gibson (trainer).
Front row: Charlie Craven, Billy Hughes, Charlie Jones, Jimmy Bye.

ABOVE: Birmingham goalkeeper Gil Merrick, who won 25 England caps and went on to manage the club.

BELOW: Eric Houghton signed for Aston Villa as a 17-year-old and played in the Villa side for two decades, scoring 170 goals in 392 games. (The total including war-time matches was over 200 goals.) He also won seven caps for England. He went on to become Aston Villa manager, guiding them to a record seventh FA Cup triumph in 1957, and after a spell managing Notts County, he returned to Villa as a director – the only person to do this at the club.

LEFT: Birmingham winger Alex Govan was always a threat in derby matches in the 1950s.

BELOW: Training at Birmingham's Elmdon ground during the 1950s.

ABOVE: Stan Lynn, seen here shepherding the ball away from Bobby Charlton during the 1957 FA Cup final, starred for both clubs in a total of 16 derby appearances. The tough-tackling full-back was also a feared penalty-taking specialist.

BELOW: Birmingham's 1956 FA Cup final team.

ABOVE: Birmingham's 1956 FA Cup final manager Arthur Turner (centre) is all smiles as chairman Harry Morris welcomes Pat Beasley as his assistant. The reality was different – Turner only learned about the appointment through the local press and resigned several months later.

RIGHT:
Peter McParland, pictured in action in 1959, played in 10 derby matches.

ABOVE: Action from the first leg of the 1963 Football League Cup final.

LEFT: How the *Daily Mirror* reported Birmingham's win.

BELOW: Action from the second leg.

ABOVE: Stan Cullis, in the centre of the picture listening to an FA Cup draw being made, came to St Andrew's with a huge reputation as the man who inspired the glory days of Wolves in the 1950s. His tenure at Birmingham was ultimately a disappointment – although his side did beat Villa 4-0 in September 1968.

RIGHT: The Blues caused controversy by going to Aston Villa to sign midfielder Ron Wylie, then aged 32 and considered past his prime, and when he then suffered a broken leg many feared his career could be over. Nevertheless, he went on to make 149 appearances, and was 37 when he retired in 1970. He then went back to Villa Park to take a job on the coaching staff.

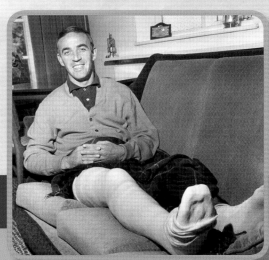

Trevor Francis, the "boy wonder" of Birmingham's 1970s side.

ABOVE: Peter Withe, seen here scoring a header for Birmingham, was a powerful centre-forward alongside Trevor Francis in the 1975–76 team and his goals helped keep them in the First Division...

BELOW: ...But he then scored three in six matches for Villa against Blues – although he will always be celebrated on the claret and blue side of town as the man who scored the goal that won the European Cup (below).

ABOVE: The "Ron Saunders derby". Villa's First Division-winning manager did his best to keep a low profile when the fixture list saw his new team Birmingham meet his former club the day after he'd taken over at St Andrew's.

LEFT: How the *Daily Mirror* reported the story.

Tempers flared in the 1983 meeting at Villa Park. Villa's Colin Gibson was sent off (above), Birmingham skipper Kevan Broadhurst was badly injured in a tackle from Steve McMahon that caused an angry reaction (below) and Noel Blake head-butted McMahon after the final whistle. He is seen walking away after the incident with McMahon on the ground in the background (bottom).

Paul Tait proved that the rivalry is never forgotten – he got fined for displaying a t-shirt that insulted Villa after scoring the golden goal that won the 1995 Auto Windscreens final.

ABOVE: Villa players show off their new kit before the 2000–01 season. Dion Dublin (centre) was sent off in a furious match against City for head-butting Robbie Savage in March 2003.

LEFT: Martin O'Neill won all four of the Premier League games he managed against Birmingham during his spell in charge – including the 5-1 victory at Villa Park which effectively doomed the Blues to relegation in April 2008.

Alex McLeish celebrates winning the Carling Cup in 2010 – victory was all the more sweet for Birmingham fans because they had beaten Aston Villa in the quarter-final.

competitive game and there was little doubt it disrupted them. After a promising start they ended the season scrapping to avoid relegation, eventually escaping by just two points after beating Leicester on the final day.

Not that Villa were without problems. They lost 11 games in a row from the end of March to the beginning of May and were grateful they already had enough points from a good start to the campaign to be clear of trouble at the foot of the table.

With those pressures out of the way, however, both sides could enjoy the fact that they had reached the League Cup final.

It is a certainty that the Blues, with the pressure lifted, looked a different team at St Andrew's as they set about building a first-leg lead.

It was a bad-tempered and physical game, however. Bobby Thomson caught goalkeeper Johnny Schofield with a bad early challenge, and Vic Crowe was just as aggressive when he caught Ken Leek with a late tackle.

Jimmy Bloomfield had to limp along on the left wing for a while because of injury, while Crowe needed treatment after receiving an elbow in the face. Doncaster referee Mr Crawford also had to split up scuffles between Charlie Aitken and Mike Hellawell.

It was winger Bertie Auld who set up Birmingham's first goal after 14 minutes, firing a centre low across goal that Leek met to turn past Nigel Sims.

It was a lead that didn't last long, however. Just before the break Harry Burrows found an opening for Thomson to beat Schofield with a well-placed shot.

Auld and Leek combined again for Birmingham's second goal just after the break, and with 66 minutes gone Bloomfield, by now sufficiently recovered from his early knock to resume at inside-right, beat two defenders on a wriggling run and held off Sims' challenge to prod the ball home.

27th May 1963

Football League Cup Final

Second Leg

Aston Villa 0

Birmingham 0

Attendance: 37,949

ASTON VILLA: *Sims, Fraser, Aitken, Crowe, Chatterley, Lee, Baker, Graham, Thomson, Wylie, Burrows*

BIRMINGHAM: *Schofield, Lynn, Green, Hennessey, Smith, Beard, Hellawell, Bloomfield, Harris, Leek, Auld*

Ever since 1956, Birmingham had been playing in the newly created Inter Cities Fairs Cup – the forerunner of the UEFA Cup and Europa League competitions.

It meant that Gil Merrick's team had superb experience of handling two-legged matches, and with a 3-1 first-leg lead they were never going to miss out on the chance to land the first major trophy in the club's 88 years of existence.

Merrick made sure his team used all the tricks they had learned from Continental opposition. Mike Hellawell took an age to find a spot on which to place the ball for corner kicks, while goalkeeper Johnny Schofield, in the words of the report of the day, "bounced the ball around merrily in the penalty area whenever he was in possession".

Birmingham's forwards also mostly adopted deeper positions as Merrick set out to get the draw which would guarantee him a place in the history books.

Villa had a reputation for staging comebacks during some of their other Cup exploits, but there was never a hint they had either the ability or the determination to do it.

Birmingham's defence, with skipper Trevor Smith in commanding form, was never seriously tested, and there were only two worthwhile efforts on goal which came from Vic Crowe and Alan Baker.

Jimmy Harris and Ken Leek missed good chances to extend the Blues' aggregate lead, but it hardly mattered.

It was another bad-tempered encounter, however. Crowe and Birmingham's Terry Hennessey were both booked as the referee fought to keep control.

But none of that mattered much to Merrick, who had crowned his long and distinguished playing service, which had included the disappointment of losing the 1956 FA Cup final, with a significant achievement as a manager.

30th March 1964

Division One
Aston Villa 0
Birmingham 3
Hellawell, Harris, Lynn (pen)
Attendance: **25,797**
ASTON VILLA: *Wilson, Fraser, Aitken, Tindall, Sleeuwenhoek, Deakin, Baker, Ewing, Hateley, Wylie, Burrows*
BIRMINGHAM: *Withers, Lynn, Green, Hennessey, Foster, Beard, Hellawell, Bloomfield, Harris, Leek, Auld*

Long-serving goalkeeper Nigel Sims, the last link to Aston Villa's 1957 FA Cup-winning team, had left the club in January after eight years' service, and manager Joe Mercer was trying to establish his replacement.

Geoff Sidebottom had half a dozen games but was then dropped after conceding four at Everton, and Mercer gave a chance to 21-year-old youth team product Bob Wilson.

Not to be confused with his namesake who played for Scotland and won the double for Arsenal, this young lad got just nine games for Villa in this season before being sold to Cardiff. Conceding six goals in two days in the Easter holidays against Birmingham probably helped make up Mercer's mind that he wasn't yet ready for first-team football.

In fact despite the scoreline of this game it was Birmingham goalkeeper Colin Withers who was the outstanding player, performing heroically as Villa dominated the first half-hour of the game.

Villa had 16 corners to Birmingham's two, yet could never make their possession count and Withers came up with brilliant stops to keep out efforts by both Mike Tindall and Alan Deakin.

Birmingham had not had a single shot on goal until the moment they took the lead after 31 minutes. Stan Lynn put a free-kick into the goalmouth and Jimmy Harris turned it into the path of Mike Hellawell for the winger to score from close range.

Harris, brought back into the team by manager Gil Merrick for only his third appearance of the season, sprang the offside trap to put the Blues two ahead just after half-time.

When Hellawell was brought down inside the box with 63 minutes gone, Lynn stepped up to hammer home the penalty and settle the result.

Villa dominated the closing stages, but Withers continued his starring display to secure relegation-threatened Birmingham's first win in 12 matches.

31st March 1964

Division One

Birmingham 3

Lynn (pen), Leek, Bloomfield

Aston Villa 3

Chatterley (2), Tindall

Attendance: 28,069

BIRMINGHAM: *Withers, Lynn, Green, Hennessey, Foster, Beard, Hellawell, Bloomfield, Harris, Leek, Auld*

ASTON VILLA: *Wilson, Fraser, Aitken, Tindall, Pountney, Deakin, Baker, Ewing, Hateley, Chatterley, Burrows*

The Football League had experimented over Easter with a return to the practice from just after the Second World War when teams played each other in back-to-back games.

So just 24 hours after losing at home to their rivals, Villa found themselves heading to St Andrew's under pressure to avoid another heavy defeat.

It was a bruising contest, with the second half in particular full of bad-tempered incidents which brought both trainers on to the pitch at regular intervals to treat injuries.

It was an exciting match, however, with Birmingham twice fighting back from behind to end up taking a point thanks to a late equalizer from Jimmy Bloomfield.

The day had started badly for Villa when John Sleeuwenhoek was ruled out by injury and a message had to be sent for Dave Pountney to rush from his home in Shropshire.

With Ron Wylie also ruled out, boss Joe Mercer took a gamble by playing reserve centre-half Lew Chatterley at inside right – and it proved a winning decision.

He put the visitors a goal up early on, pouncing on a chance after Birmingham keeper Colin Withers had scrambled away a diagonal shot from Alan Baker.

Baker also supplied the second goal, picking out Mike Tindall with a neat pass before the right-half let loose a shot from 20 yards.

The game swung almost immediately – Bertie Auld ran trickily from the wing and was brought down by Pountney, giving Lynn the chance to convert yet another derby penalty.

Then Ken Leek equalized, heading the ball home from a Mike Hellawell cross.

The action was hectic, Chatterley scoring his second after just 30 minutes when he was perfectly positioned to score after good work from Tommy Ewing.

After the break the game got increasingly physical, and it was just beginning to look as if Villa would hold on to their lead when, with a minute to go, Bloomfield pushed the ball beyond a defender, sprinted clear and then let go his shot.

It was to prove a vital goal – Birmingham ended the season avoiding relegation by a single point.

13th February 1965

Division One
Birmingham 0
Aston Villa 1
Stobart
Attendance: 32,491
BIRMINGHAM: *Schofield, Lynn, Green, Page, Foster, Beard, Jackson, Sharples, Fenton, Vowden, Thwaites*
ASTON VILLA: *Withers, Bradley, Aitken, Wylie, Pountney, Deakin, MacEwan, Stobart, Hateley, Woosnam, Burrows*

Joe Mercer stood down as Aston Villa manager through ill health during the summer of 1964, and the directors decided to appoint from within, promoting his assistant Dick Taylor.

As a sign of their faith in the new man, Villa's board backed him to break their transfer record early in his reign, paying £40,000 to sign Arsenal winger John MacLeod.

But the ambition was not backed up by performances, and by the time derby day came round in February, the team were struggling at the wrong end of the table.

Meanwhile the Blues, who had also changed managers at the start of the campaign by ditching Gil Merrick, were having just as bad a time under his replacement Joe Mallett, so both teams were under pressure.

MacLeod was missing injured, and Villa had to make another late change giving 18-year-old Keith Bradley a debut at right-back when Michael Wright failed a fitness test two hours before kick-off.

The pressure made it a dour clash, with the two sides scared of making mistakes. Birmingham, who had a completely different forward line to the one which had contested the previous derby 11 months earlier, were especially guilty of putting too much emphasis on making sure they didn't lose, rather than trying to win the game.

In the event it was settled by a goalkeeping mistake. Just before half-time Johnny Schofield came off his line to collect a cross from Barry Stobart, misjudged it in the wind, and the ball swirled above his head and into the net.

The Blues responded well after the break, creating pressure, but goalkeeper Colin Withers kept them out with superb saves from both Dennis Thwaites and Stan Lynn.

12th April 1965

Division One

Aston Villa 3

Woosnam, Chatterley, Hateley

Birmingham 0

Attendance: 36,871

BIRMINGHAM: Schofield, Lynn, Green, Hennessey, Foster, Sharples, Jackson, Bullock, Vowden, Fraser, Thwaites

ASTON VILLA: Withers, Bradley, Aitken, Wylie, Pountney, Deakin, Baker, Chatterley, Hateley, Woosnam, MacLeod

With both teams still embroiled in a relegation fight as the season moved towards its climax, Blues manager Joe Mallett took a massive gamble in his team selection.

A win would take them above Villa on goal difference with four games left, and after losing the first derby of the season by being too negative, Mallett opted to go on the attack.

He decided to switch full-back Stan Lynn to play as part of the forward line, asking Cammie Fraser to switch to a deeper role even though he was wearing the number 10 shirt.

The plan backfired – within 11 minutes they were a goal down as a long ball bounced down the middle of a disorganized defence and Phil Woosnam was quickest to get to it, lobbing the ball over the top of the advancing Johnny Schofield.

The home team had barely recovered from that when they went two down, as Lew Chatterley met Ron Wylie's cross with a thumping header – celebrating by taking the ball from the net and carrying it above his head back to the centre circle.

The Blues managed to cause a couple of scares for their former goalkeeper Colin Withers just before the break. He kept out a low shot from Dennis Thwaites and then held on to a good shot from Brian Sharples when Villa failed to defend a corner kick.

But the plan to exploit Lynn's physical power up front didn't work, with the service to him not good enough.

Villa could have scored more after the break. Tony Hateley missed three good chances before finally reaching a centre from Alan Baker to put a trademark header beyond Schofield's reach.

It was a pivotal result for both clubs. Villa went unbeaten for the remainder of the campaign to end up well clear of trouble, while the Blues took just two more points and finished bottom.

7th October 1967

Division Two

Aston Villa 2

Greenhalgh, Godfrey

Birmingham 4

Bridges (2), Beard (pen), Vowden

Attendance: 50,067

ASTON VILLA: *Withers, Bradley, Aitken, Chatterley, Sleeuwenhoek, Tindall, Rudge (Park), Broadbent, Greenhalgh, Godfrey, Anderson*

BIRMINGHAM: *Herriot, Murray, Green, Wylie, Page, Beard, Bridges, Vincent, Pickering, Vowden, Hockey*

If any Aston Villa fans had celebrated pushing Birmingham through the relegation trapdoor, then two years later they were taking their own turn to suffer.

The decision to accept a £100,000 transfer fee from Chelsea for centre-forward Tony Hateley the previous season had backfired horribly and ended in relegation – meaning for the first time a second city derby had become a Second Division contest.

Crowds had plummeted at Villa Park in response to the loss of status, with just 13,673 watching their first home match of the season against Rotherham.

But the lure of the old enemy brought fans flocking back for this game with more than 50,000 packed into the ground and the Holte End heaving with enthusiastic supporters.

Villa's new manager was former Burnley defender Tommy Cummings, and he had just signed Preston forwards Brian Godfrey and Brian Greenhalgh in a combined deal worth £35,000.

The pair had made their debuts in a 1-1 draw at Middlesbrough a week earlier, with Godfrey scoring, and Villa's fans were looking forward to seeing their new strike force.

It took just four minutes for Greenhalgh to get his first goal for the club, meeting Willie Anderson's left-wing cross with a header that crept just inside the post.

The Blues hit back with a spectacular overhead kick by Barry Bridges following a 21st-minute long throw by Geoff Vowden that caught the home defence napping.

But when Godfrey got on the end of a John Rudge cross with half an hour gone, it looked like it was destined to be a glory day for the two Villa new boys.

Instead, Birmingham were let back into the game by a disputed penalty that Malcolm Beard scored, and shortly after half-time Ron Wylie began a move that ended with Vowden scoring.

There had been several bad-tempered scuffles during the game, and the second half remained tense until with nine minutes remaining Wylie began another move that ended with Bridges stabbing the ball home from close range.

24th February 1968

Division Two
Birmingham 2
Bridges (2)
Aston Villa 1
Godfrey
Attendance: 45,283
BIRMINGHAM: *Herriot, Martin, Green, Wylie, Foster, Beard, Bridges, Vincent, Pickering, Vowden, Page*
ASTON VILLA: *Withers, Bradley, Aitken, Deakin, Chatterley, Park, Roberts, Mitchinson, Woodward, Godfrey, Anderson*

Birmingham's ambition to regain their First Division status couldn't be faulted – they persuaded Stan Cullis, the manager who had inspired Wolves' great era in the 1950s, to come out of retirement and they backed him with money to rebuild the team.

One of his major signings was Chelsea striker Barry Bridges, one of several players in the Swinging Sixties era at Stamford Bridge who fell out of favour with manager Tommy Docherty after being caught breaking a curfew.

He took time to settle, however, getting just 13 League goals in his first season after Cullis decided to switch him to the wings rather than play him at centre-forward.

But he then adapted to the role and got 22 in this campaign, although a lack of support from other strikers meant that the Blues finished up six points short of winning promotion.

He was certainly the match-winner in this game, getting both goals as Cullis' team completed a double over their local rivals who were more concerned about staying up than going up as the disappointment of dropping into the Second Division spilled into another poor campaign.

Bridges had been a sprint champion in his schoolboy days and he couldn't have got the Blues off to a quicker start.

Just 17 seconds had been played when he ran on to Geoff Vowden's perfectly weighted through-ball and hit a first-time shot that flashed beyond the reach of goalkeeper Colin Withers.

The Blues wasted a good chance to make it 2-0 just before half-time as a Johnny Vincent shot was hooked off the line by Charlie Aitken and Vowden fired wide of an open goal.

Almost immediately they were punished for the miss, as Brian Godfrey equalized after a Keith Bradley lob had been helped on by John Woodward.

But, roared on by a big crowd, Birmingham dominated the second half and deserved to win the game as Bridges again used his pace to get clear of Villa's defence for the winner.

21st September 1968

Division Two

Birmingham 4

Summerill, Vincent, Greenhoff, Vowden

Aston Villa 0

Attendance: 40,527

BIRMINGHAM: *Herriot, Martin, Page, Wylie, Robinson, Beard, Hockey, Greenhoff, Vowden, Vincent, Summerill*

ASTON VILLA: *Withers, Wright, Aitken, Edwards, Turnbull, Hole, Ferguson, Greenhalgh, Woodward, Godfrey, Anderson*

The first signs of the hooliganism which would blight English football in the 1970s and '80s were beginning to emerge – and this derby day brought out the worst.

Supporters from both clubs had been praised for their behaviour in the two derbies the previous season, but the tension surrounding this match after both clubs had got off to a bad start in the season created a bad atmosphere.

After just five minutes' play the referee, Mr Dave Smith from Gloucestershire, stopped the game while he asked officials to make an appeal over the loudspeakers to warn that "drastic action" would be taken if more stones were thrown into the Villa goalmouth.

Crowd behaviour improved but it remained a bad afternoon for Villa's goalkeeper Colin Withers, and it turned out to be the last of his 163 games for the club.

Having survived that first barrage he then faced missiles of a different kind as Birmingham smashed four goals past him and ran out emphatic winners.

Villa had got off to an awful start to the season with just five points from the first nine games, causing manager Tommy Cummings to make a plea to supporters to lay off the players and direct any criticism at him.

Just to add to the pre-match problems Lew Chatterley put in a transfer request in protest at being left out of the team.

Birmingham manager Stan Cullis had made another big-money buy to chase promotion, paying £70,000 to Leeds for Jimmy Greenhoff – and it paid immediate dividends.

He had already scored three in his first four games and was the star player in a superb second-half display, setting up the opening goal for winger Phil Summerill and then scoring himself as Villa's defence fell to pieces.

Johnny Vincent and Geoff Vowden got the other goals on a day that effectively ended Cummings' 18-month reign as Villa manager – he was sacked six weeks later with the club still in the relegation zone.

12th April 1969

Division Two

Aston Villa 1

Simmons

Birmingham 0

Attendance: 53,647

ASTON VILLA: *Dunn, Bradley, Aitken, Hole, Edwards, Chatterley, Ferguson, Godfrey, Simmons, Tiler, Anderson*

BIRMINGHAM: *D. Latchford, Page, Thomson, Wylie, Robinson, Pendrey, Vowden, Vincent, Pickering, Hockey, Summerill*

It was a very different Aston Villa team that played the second derby of the season – transformed by the arrival of the colourful and controversial figure of Tommy Docherty as manager.

He had been appointed within a few days of Doug Ellis becoming chairman in December, and immediately set about a whirlwind transformation of the club.

He signed Brian Tiler from Rotherham for £35,000 and completely changed the team so that only six players from the first meeting were still in the team by this time.

It brought initial success – a run of just one defeat in 17 games steered Villa well clear of the relegation zone, even though they had been bottom when Tommy Cummings and his assistant Malcolm Musgrove were dismissed.

They underlined that improvement with a superb display against Birmingham at Villa Park, showing tenacity and determination to secure their first derby win in more than four years.

In fact it was Birmingham's young goalkeeper Dave Latchford, brought into the team for a surprise debut a week earlier in a 2-1 win at Bury, who was the star of the show.

Latchford, who had been in the club's FA Youth Cup final side two years earlier, was only three days past his 20th birthday, but played with great courage to defy Villa's attacks.

He made excellent saves from both Tiler and Mike Ferguson, and was unlucky to be beaten by the Dave Simmons goal in the 55th minute which settled the game.

Latchford pulled off another brilliant save to get his fingers to a Dick Edwards header after he had been left unmarked at a free-kick, but in the scramble that followed, Simmons stabbed the ball over the line.

18th October 1969

Division Two
Aston Villa 0
Birmingham 0
Attendance: **54,405**
ASTON VILLA: *Phillips, Wright, Aitken, Tiler, Edwards, Chatterley, Ferguson, Godfrey, Martin, B. Rioch, Anderson*
BIRMINGHAM: *Herriot, Martin, Thomson, Beard, Sleeuwenhoek, Pendrey, Murray, Vowden, Hateley, Hockey, Summerill*

Villa started the season with the most expensive side in the Second Division, having spent more than £200,000 on new players including £110,000 for brothers Bruce and Neil Rioch from Luton and £40,000 for "Chico" Hamilton from Southend.

But Tommy Docherty's spending spree had anything but the desired result and Villa were stuck at the foot of the table after 14 matches with only two wins.

Docherty's response had been to spend more money – the latest dip into the transfer market was a £30,000 move to sign 18-year-old goalkeeper John Phillips from Shrewsbury.

The teenager was thrown into the hothouse atmosphere of a derby for his debut but coped brilliantly with the occasion and made the one big save of the game when after 79 minutes he threw himself bravely at the feet of Bert Murray when a goal seemed certain.

Referee Leo Callaghan set the tone for the game by booking Garry Pendrey and Lionel Martin after just three minutes.

Pendrey, a feisty competitor who had been appointed captain of Birmingham at the age of just 20, settled to produce an excellent performance and began the move which brought Birmingham's best chance when former Villa centre-forward Tony Hateley hit the post with a header.

There was controversy as Birmingham thought they should have had two penalties after Mark Wright appeared to trip Phil Summerill, and then Hateley was bundled over in the area late in the game.

Certainly Villa did little to deserve more than a point. Bruce Rioch struck a couple of optimistic long-range shots but never really troubled Birmingham keeper Jim Herriot.

30th March 1970

Division Two

Birmingham 0

Aston Villa 2

B. Rioch, McMahon

Attendance: **41,696**

BIRMINGHAM: *D. Latchford, Martin, Thomson, Hockey, Sleeuwenhoek, Beard, Murray, Page, Hateley, Vincent, Summerill*

ASTON VILLA: *Dunn, Wright, Aitken, Tiler, Curtis, Chatterley, McMahon, B. Rioch, Lochhead, Hamilton, Anderson*

A season that had started full of optimism was ending disastrously. Villa were on their way into the third tier for the only time in the club's history. Tommy Docherty had been sacked in January with his assistant Vic Crowe appointed to replace him, but it had done little to change the fortunes of a team that was not functioning and were rooted to the foot of the table with time running out.

Yet it was typical that derby day should bring arguably the best performance of the season – their only away win of the entire campaign.

It was Bruce Rioch, the club's record signing, who finally hit the sort of form that had persuaded Docherty to spend £100,000 on him.

He struck a tremendous 14th-minute volley that put Villa on their way to victory – a great strike from 25 yards after a Willie Anderson corner had been headed away by Trevor Hockey.

Villa continued to dominate, with their former defender John Sleeuwenhoek needing to give an assured performance to keep the attacking flair of Andy Lochhead and Chico Hamilton at bay.

But with nine minutes left Anderson centred from wide on the left, Lochhead let the ball go, and Pat McMahon came running in to clinch the result.

"Where there's life, there's hope," said chairman Doug Ellis afterwards – he was also celebrating backing a 9-1 winner at Market Rasen races earlier in the day. "We have by no means given up hope of avoiding relegation."

Meanwhile manager Crowe insisted: "I am pleased we won, but more pleased at the way in which we won. This victory was convincing, good for our morale, and it will renew the faith, confidence and pride of both the team and our supporters."

His side did go on to take two wins and a draw from their last four matches, but it was too little and far too late.

Chapter Seven

The 1970s

If the 1960s had been a let-down, the next decade was to bring arguably the most vibrant ever period for football in the Midlands.

Birmingham and Aston Villa both went through spells of exciting regeneration, and to add to the flamboyant atmosphere, it was a time when West Bromwich Albion and Wolves were also playing audacious, attacking football. The players were stars across a city which embraced its football heroes.

When Stan Cullis stepped down as Birmingham manager, the directors talked about getting big names like Brian Clough, Don Revie or Ronnie Allen. That didn't happen – and there was disappointment when instead they appointed Freddie Goodwin, a former Manchester United player who had gone to the States to cut his management teeth in the emerging North American Soccer League.

It proved inspired. Goodwin arrived with ideas which were years ahead of their time, developing psychological testing to create a more scientific approach to team-building, introducing yoga to the players' training regime to combat injuries, and paying attention to diet. At Birmingham's Elmdon training ground he worked on team shape and tactics, and formed a side which was to win promotion back to the First Division in 1972.

He also took a chance by picking a raw 16-year-old by the name of Trevor Francis as substitute for a game at Cardiff – and in the process discovered the player who would be the symbol of the next decade. The Blues fans identified with the swashbuckling kid who played without fear, as Francis tapped into their support to play with super confidence, and the team around him flourished.

Villa had hit rock-bottom under Tommy Docherty's controversial reign, although it was his replacement Vic Crowe who was in charge when relegation to the Third Division was confirmed. Crowe, who had played for Villa for 10 years from 1954, set about the task of rebuilding. Though there was disappointment when they managed only fourth place in their first year among the minnows, he raised hopes by taking the side to Wembley in the League Cup final thanks to an exciting semi-final win over two legs against Manchester United.

The next season they took the Third Division by storm, with average gates of more than 32,000 to cheer a new group of players for whom centre-forward Andy Lochhead led the way with 19 League goals.

Across town the Blues were breaking records – their deal to sign Howard Kendall and Archie Styles from Everton in a swap with Bob Latchford was valued at a British record £350,000. And Goodwin's forward line of Francis, Bob Hatton and Bob Latchford was a match on its day for any side in the First Division. Goodwin's side came agonizingly close to a return to Wembley in the FA Cup, losing in a semi-final replay in the last minute of extra-time to a Bobby Moore-inspired Fulham team.

Villa needed to keep up. After failing to build on his first promotion, Vic Crowe was sacked and Ron Saunders appointed. His attention to physical fitness and organization brought immediate dividends and Villa not only won the League Cup twice – beating Norwich at Wembley with a goal by Ray Graydon then Everton two years later after two enthralling replays – but clinched promotion back to the First Division with an all-conquering side that won eight games in a row.

Saunders loved work and discipline but had flair players like Brian Little in his side, and showed his ability to spot talent by paying £110,000 for centre-forward Andy Gray from Dundee United. The 19-year-old took English football by storm. He was big, aggressive, fearless, and Villa's fans loved their new centre-forward as the team finished fourth in the First Division in 1977 and won the League Cup yet again.

Skipper Dennis Mortimer was to say that the success in the League Cup during this decade was vital for the club – a catalyst that got the players into the habit of winning trophies and paved the way for the glories that were to come in the early 1980s.

Sadly for the Blues their neighbours had not just caught them up, but overtaken them. A brief period with Sir Alf Ramsey in charge, the man who won the World Cup for England in 1966, ended in a row over whether Trevor Francis should be sold. His successor Jim Smith was the man who eventually negotiated the game's first £1million transfer, and without their talisman Birmingham slipped towards another relegation.

Record in the 1970s

Aston Villa:

Season	League	P	W	D	L	F	A	Pts	Position
1970–71	Div 3	46	19	15	12	54	46	53	4
1971–72	Div 3	46	32	6	8	85	32	70	1
1972–73	Div 2	42	18	14	10	51	47	50	3
1973–74	Div 2	42	13	15	14	48	51	41	14
1974–75	Div 2	42	25	8	9	79	32	58	2
1975–76	Div 1	42	11	17	14	51	59	39	16
1976–77	Div 1	42	22	7	13	76	50	51	4
1977–78	Div 1	42	18	10	14	57	42	46	8
1978–79	Div 1	42	15	16	11	59	49	46	8
1979–80	Div 1	42	16	14	12	51	50	46	7

FA Cup

1970–71   1-3 v Torquay United (first round)
1971–72   0-1 v Southend United (first round)

1972–73	1-3 v Everton (third round)
1973–74	0-1 v Burnley (fifth round)
1974–75	2-3 v Ipswich Town (fifth round)
1975–76	1-1, 1-2 v Southampton (third round)
1976–77	1-2 v Manchester United (sixth round)
1977–78	1-4 v Everton (third round)
1978–79	0-2 v Nottingham Forest (third round)
1979–80	0-1 v West Ham United (sixth round)

Football League Cup

1970–71	0-2 v Tottenham Hotspur (final at Wembley Stadium)
1971–72	1-4 v Blackpool (fourth round)
1972–73	1-1, 0-2 v Leeds United (third round)
1973–74	0-1 v York City (second round)
1974–75	1-0 v Norwich (final at Wembley Stadium)
1975–76	1-2 v Manchester United (third round)
1976–77	0-0, 1-1, 3-2 v Everton (final at Wembley Stadium, replays at Hillsborough and Old Trafford
1977–78	2-4 v Nottingham Forest (fourth round)
1978–79	0-2 v Luton Town (fourth round)
1979–80	0-0, 1-4 v Everton (third round)

European Competition

1975–76	UEFA Cup 0-4, 0-1 to Royal Antwerp (first round)
1976–77	did not qualify
1977–78	UEFA Cup 2-2, 1-2 to Barcelona (fourth round)
1978–79	did not qualify
1979–80	did not qualify

Birmingham:

Season	League	P	W	D	L	F	A	Pts	Position
1970–71	Div 2	42	17	12	13	58	48	46	9
1971–72	Div 2	42	19	18	5	60	31	56	2

1972–73	Div 1	42	15	12	15	53	54	42	10
1973–74	Div 1	42	12	13	17	52	64	37	19
1974–75	Div 1	42	14	9	19	53	61	37	17
1975–76	Div 1	42	13	7	22	57	75	33	19
1976–77	Div 1	42	13	12	17	63	61	38	13
1977–78	Div 1	42	16	9	17	55	60	41	11
1978–79	Div 1	42	6	10	26	37	64	22	21
1979–80	Div 2	42	21	11	10	58	38	53	3

FA Cup

1970–71	1-1, 0-2 v Huddersfield Town (third round)
1971–72	0-3 v Leeds United (semi-final)
1972–73	0-2 v Swindon Town (third round)
1973–74	0-2 v Queens Park Rangers (fourth round)
1974–75	1-1, 0-1 v Fulham (semi-final)
1975–76	1-1, 0-1 v Portsmouth (third round)
1976–77	1-2 v Leeds United (fourth round)
1977–78	1-2 v Derby County (fourth round)
1978–79	0-2 v Burnley (third round)
1979–80	1-3 v Tottenham Hotspur (fifth round)

Football League Cup

1970–71	0-3 v Bristol Rovers (fourth round)
1971–72	0-2 v Queens Park Rangers (second round)
1972–73	0-2 v Blackpool (fourth round)
1973–74	1-2 v Plymouth (fifth round)
1974–75	1-2 v Crewe Alexandra (second round)
1975–76	0-2 v Wolverhampton Wanderers (third round)
1976–77	1-2 v Blackpool (second round)
1977–78	0-2 v Notts County (second round)
1978–79	2-5 v Southampton (second round)
1979–80	1-2 v Exeter City (third round)

27th September 1975

Division One

Aston Villa 2

Hamilton, Little

Birmingham 1

Francis

Attendance: 53,782

ASTON VILLA: *Burridge, Gidman, Aitken, Ross, Nicholl, Phillips, Graydon, Little, Robson, Hamilton, Carrodus*

BIRMINGHAM: *D. Latchford, Osborne, Want, Kendall, Gallagher, Burns, Campbell, Francis, Withe (Pendrey), Hatton, Hibbitt*

Much had changed in the five years since the last derby. Freddie Goodwin had led Birmingham back into the First Division with a side built around the precocious talent of teenager Trevor Francis – only to lose his job after taking two points from the first seven games of this season; Villa had climbed from the depths of the Third Division to return to the top flight under the guidance of Ron Saunders.

Acting manager Willie Bell had demanded greater commitment to stop the rot and got wins over Burnley and Newcastle in his first two games.

But with so much pride at stake the result was a brutal encounter of 39 fouls – 18 of them committed by either Kenny Burns or Joe Gallagher as the Blues adopted a physical approach to the game.

It left Villa with seven players needing treatment, four days before they were due to play Royal Antwerp in the second leg of a UEFA Cup tie, and captain Ian Ross furious at Burns for one particular tackle on John Robson.

Ross claimed: "That was the worst tackle I have seen. If one of my players had done that I would have told him he shouldn't be playing football and wouldn't have spoken to him for a week."

And Frank Carrodus said: "I don't think I was tackled once when I had the ball, it was always after it had gone. It was ridiculous, I don't know which leg to limp on."

The conditions added to the drama of the contest – one minute drenching rain and the next bright sunshine.

The Blues appeared to be well on their way to winning after Francis gave them the lead in the 12th minute, but the game changed when Peter Withe had to go off injured just before half-time.

Goalkeeper Dave Latchford had to make two smart saves to deny Ray Graydon and then Brian Little, but could do nothing when John Robson headed on for Chico Hamilton to score from close range.

It was a mistake by Burns which led to the winner – he lost control and Little nipped in to curve a shot beyond Latchford's reach.

Blues might have got an equalizer, but John Burridge, making his debut after a £90,000 move from Blackpool, saved brilliantly from Francis in the final minutes.

3rd April 1976

Division One
Birmingham 3
Hibbitt, Burns, Francis
Aston Villa 2
Gray, Graydon (pen)
Attendance: 46,251
BIRMINGHAM: *D. Latchford, Calderwood, Styles, Kendall, Gallagher (Hatton), Want, Emmanuel, Francis, Burns, Needham, Hibbitt*
ASTON VILLA: *Burridge, Gidman, Robson, Ross, Nicholl, Mortimer, Graydon, Little, Gray, Hamilton, Carrodus*

Willie Bell's promotion from player-coach to manager had helped lift Birmingham away from the foot of the First Division but they were still flirting with relegation as the season reached its climax.

He'd come to realize, though, that local pride and the knock-on effect of a successful performance in the big derby was every bit as important as the points at stake.

He'd watched Ron Saunders' side revive their fortunes with just three defeats in 12 games following their win at Villa Park earlier in the campaign.

And with his side still too close to the foot of the table for comfort he knew he could get a similar boost from a successful rematch at St Andrew's.

"Before the last game I went on record as saying it was just another game, because being a Scot from outside of this area I was not really aware of what it meant to people," he admitted.

"Now I am as keen to win this game as anyone else, not only because of the points at stake but because of the local rivalry."

He got his wish. Villa caused his side trouble in the first half, with 20-year-old Andy Gray's physical power at centre-forward making life tough for centre-half Joe Gallagher.

Goals by Gray and Terry Hibbitt made it one each at half-time, and it stayed tight after the break with Kenny Burns scoring for Blues, but a Ray Graydon penalty keeping things level.

With time running out 21-year-old Trevor Francis gave a glimpse of the pace and finishing prowess that brought him 17 goals this season as he raced on to a loose ball and got there just before John Burridge to prod home the winner.

18th September 1976

Division One

Aston Villa 1

Gray

Birmingham 2

Burns, Connolly

Attendance: 50,084

ASTON VILLA: *Burridge, Gidman, Smith, Phillips, Nicholl, Mortimer, Graydon, Little, Gray, Robson (Hunt), Carrodus*

BIRMINGHAM: *D. Latchford, Page, Styles, Kendall (Calderwood), Gallagher, Want, Jones, Francis, Burns, Hibbitt, Connolly*

Birmingham began the season by losing centre-forward Peter Withe, lured to Nottingham Forest by the prospect of working with Brian Clough.

Manager Willie Bell's answer was to look within his ranks and switch tough-guy defender Kenny Burns from playing at centre-half to centre-forward.

It was a decision that was to prove a spectacular success as alongside Trevor Francis he gave the team a twin-pronged attacking force that caused problems to any opposition – they were to end this season sharing 40 goals between them.

Bell had actually begun the experiment in the derby the previous season, and Villa were on the receiving end of the Scot's ability yet again.

Villa began the game in great heart – a huge crowd letting loose claret and blue balloons and giving a rousing reception to manager Ron Saunders as he collected his Manager of the Month award for August.

Saunders waved his bottle of Scotch to the Holte End, and must have felt more than happy as his side took control of the game and went into an early lead.

There were 13 minutes gone when Brian Little's anticipation helped him cash in on a mistake by Terry Hibbitt to gain possession, and he went on a run beating three men before knocking the ball into the goalmouth to where Andy Gray was steaming in to force it over the line.

Villa should have increased that lead – instead Burns wiped it out after 29 minutes. Francis used his acceleration to get clear on the left, and when Chris Nicholl failed to clear his cross Burns got on the end of it to score.

Just before half-time John Connolly, recruited two weeks earlier from Everton for £90,000, came up with a wonderful individual goal.

He beat Chris Nicholl to win the ball some 45 yards out, then evaded two tackles as he sprinted on before placing a shot perfectly beyond the reach of John Burridge.

10th May 1977

Division One
Birmingham 2
Hibbitt, Francis (pen)
Aston Villa 1
Deehan
Attendance: 43,721
BIRMINGHAM: *Latchford D, Calderwood, Pendrey, Page, Gallagher, Sbragia, Jones, Francis, Burns, Hibbitt, Connolly*
ASTON VILLA: *Burridge, Smith, Robson, Phillips, Nicholl, Mortimer, Deehan, Little, Gray, Cropley, Cowans*

Leighton Phillips and Joe Gallagher became the first players to be sent off in 90 years and 85 competitive second city matches in a stormy St Andrew's encounter.

The feuds that had built up across two seasons finally exploded in an ugly encounter as Birmingham scored a win that ended their fears of getting sucked into the relegation fight.

Even the winning goal was surrounded by anger and controversy. With 10 minutes left Trevor Francis tumbled over an Andy Gray challenge before dusting himself off to score from the spot, while Villa claimed referee Peter Reeves had been conned into awarding the kick.

The result made Birmingham the only side to do the double over Villa in a season where Ron Saunders' gradually emerging side finished fourth and won the League Cup after two thrilling replays against Everton.

The bad-tempered tone was set as early as the fifth minute when Terry Hibbitt and Gordon Cowans clashed with each other while Garry Pendrey got into another row with Brian Little.

Pendrey might have been booked earlier than the 22nd minute when he tripped John Deehan to stop him breaking through – and eight minutes after that Phillips ploughed into a heavy tackle from behind on Francis.

The Welsh international was booked for the tackle and kicked the ball away, and when referee Reeves told him to fetch it he appeared to aim a V-sign at the official and got a red card in return.

Remarkably Villa's 10 men took the lead thanks to a magnificent headed goal by Deehan from Dennis Mortimer's cross.

Francis then produced a moment of magic to level the scores, holding off the challenge of both Chris Nicholl and John Robson before rolling the ball into the path of Hibbitt for the midfielder to curl a low shot beyond the reach of John Burridge.

That sparked another explosion – three minutes later Gallagher appeared to aim a kick at Deehan while he lay on the ground following a collision between the pair.

There were angry protests about that decision – and more when Gray, switched into emergency duty in defence in the reshuffle that followed the first red card, was tempted into the collision with Francis which led to the decisive penalty.

1st October 1977

Division One
Aston Villa 0
Birmingham 1
Bertschin
Attendance: **45,436**
ASTON VILLA: *Rimmer, Gidman, Smith, Phillips, Gregory, Mortimer, Deehan, Little, Cowans, Cropley, Carrodus*
BIRMINGHAM: *Montgomery, Calderwood, Pendrey, Towers, Howard, Want, Broadbent, Francis, Bertschin, Hibbitt, Emmanuel*

Sir Alf Ramsey, the man who won the World Cup for England a decade earlier, had been invited to join Birmingham City's board back in January 1976 to use his experience to support Willie Bell.

At the time both he and Birmingham's chairman Clifford Coombs insisted there were no plans for Sir Alf to involve himself in first-team affairs.

But when another season started with four successive defeats and Bell was dismissed it was inevitable that he would take the reins, if only as caretaker.

He insisted: "I will only do this job until a permanent manager is signed, because there is not much future in me at 57."

But then he immediately proved that the old magic was still there, organizing the team to achieve victories over Middlesbrough and Newcastle, and although a trip to West Brom ended in a 3-1 defeat there was a new optimism about the side as they travelled to Villa Park.

Sir Alf made few changes to the team he took over, but more than that he simply gave them confidence and they produced a display of great defensive discipline to keep Villa's forwards at bay after Keith Bertschin had grabbed the 36th-minute winning goal.

It was the third goal in as many games scored by the former Ipswich striker, signed during the summer for £135,000, and he gave the credit to the club's temporary boss.

And while Sir Alf insisted to reporters afterwards: "I have done very little", Bertschin told a different story.

He said: "He believes in himself and we believe in him. Before we went out to play at Villa Park there was a definite air of 'over-our-dead-bodies'."

25th February 1978

Division One

Birmingham 1

Francis

Aston Villa 0

Attendance: 33,679

BIRMINGHAM: *Montgomery, Calderwood, Styles, Towers, Gallagher, Howard, Fox (Page), Francis, Bertschin, Hibbitt, Dillon*

ASTON VILLA: *Rimmer, Gidman (Gregory), Smith, Phillips, McNaught, Mortimer, Craig, Little, Deehan, Cowans, Carrodus*

Birmingham gained bragging rights yet again as they won the second city derby for the fifth time in a row – but lady luck was on their side.

Somehow Villa managed to hit the woodwork no fewer than four times and miss a hatful of other chances and were then punished when Trevor Francis got the only goal in the 59th minute.

Sir Alf Ramsey could claim it wasn't only that goalkeeper Jim Montgomery led a charmed life, however. His team also produced a disciplined display in defence.

The team spirit they showed was all the more remarkable because there was trouble behind the scenes. Francis and Joe Gallagher had both asked for transfers in the days leading up to the game, yet both gave performances of total commitment.

John Deehan was the Villa striker who missed out, twice hitting the post with headers, while Brian Little and Gordon Cowans were the others to be denied by the woodwork.

An added concern for Ron Saunders was that reliable defender John Gidman was carried off injured after 30 minutes, forcing him to miss the first leg of a UEFA Cup tie against Barcelona four days later.

And if they needed proof it was not to be their day it came when Jimmy Rimmer failed to hold on to a fairly harmless long shot and Francis reacted at the speed of light to grab his 17th goal of the season.

Ramsey was ready to sell him to use the cash for strengthening other parts of the team, only for Birmingham's board to decide a week later that their biggest star must stay, provoking Sir Alf to resign and walk away from the club and football altogether.

21st October 1978

Division One
Birmingham 0
Aston Villa 1
Gray
Attendance: 36,145
BIRMINGHAM: *Montgomery, Broadbent, Dennis, Tarantini, Gallagher, Pendrey, Page, Buckley, Givens, Emmanuel, Barrowclough*
ASTON VILLA: *Rimmer, Gidman, Williams, Evans, McNaught, Mortimer, Craig, Little, Gray, Gregory, Young*

Tottenham manager Keith Burkinshaw stunned English football during the summer by flying to Argentina and snapping up two members of their World Cup-winning side, Ossie Ardiles and Ricky Villa.

It was a breathtaking swoop, and Birmingham boss Jim Smith was one of many who admired the attempt to introduce some South American flair to the First Division.

He won backing from the Blues board to make his own trip into the Argentine transfer market, paying £295,000 to get defender Alberto Tarantini from Boca Juniors.

The long-haired star ironically made his debut at White Hart Lane up against Ardiles and Villa, but a week later was back at St Andrew's for Birmingham's home fans to see him for the first time.

It was a promising display with some skilful touches, and he came close to crowning his performance with a goal just after half-time when an Allan Evans header went to him and he fired a first-time volley that flew an inch wide of the post.

But the day belonged to Villa, for whom Evans was in immaculate form in defence alongside Ken McNaught in the partnership that would go on to win the European Cup.

The goal which brought Villa's first win at St Andrew's in a First Division game since 1965 came after only eight minutes.

Andy Gray rounded off a breakaway attack, sprinting clear to beat Jim Montgomery with a cool piece of finishing.

Mark Dennis and Gary Emmanuel of Birmingham were both booked in a match that was as fiercely fought as any derby, although thankfully both teams maintained control of their tempers.

3rd March 1979

Division One
Aston Villa 1
Cowans
Birmingham 0
Attendance: 42,419
ASTON VILLA: *Rimmer, Gidman, Williams, Gregory, Evans, Mortimer, Craig, Little, Gray, Cowans, Swain*
BIRMINGHAM: *Freeman, Page, Dennis, Towers, Gallagher, Tarantini, Ainscow, Bertschin, Givens, Dillon, Broadhurst*

The coldest winter since 1963 had hit Villa hard – in the days before under-soil heating they had not been able to play a single home game between Boxing Day and the start of March when the Blues arrived at Villa Park.

The fates were kinder to Birmingham who had not had a game postponed during February, but their season was suffering just as much ill fortune through injury.

Keith Bertschin suffered a broken leg after only three matches, Trevor Francis also suffered several long absences, and manager

Jim Smith was never able to field a settled side.

Bertschin was just beginning to return to fitness by the time this game came around, but lacked both sharpness and a forward partner as the club had made Francis the game's first £1million player when they sold him to Nottingham Forest three weeks earlier.

Without a goal threat, the Blues had got deep into relegation trouble. A 2-1 win at Tottenham the week before this game had ended a dismal run of eight League defeats in a row.

But Smith's team showed great character and determination as they set about trying to see if they could make Villa suffer from the lack of match fitness.

The result was another dour encounter, with Villa's John Gregory and Kevin Dillon both booked in the first half, while Malcolm Page and Joe Gallagher also had their names taken after the interval.

Gallagher was effective organizing a defence that looked happy to settle for a point and mostly kept Andy Gray and Brian Little under control.

But with 10 minutes to go Gallagher didn't get enough power when he tried to head the ball clear, and it fell for Gordon Cowans to crack an unstoppable shot from 15 yards that gave goalkeeper Neil Freeman no chance.

Chapter Eight

The 1980s

Ron Saunders had already proved his ability to wheel and deal, but his greatest bit of transfer juggling had dramatic consequences.

As the 1970s came to a close he accepted an astonishing bid of £1,469,000 from Wolves for centre-forward Andy Gray, then started ploughing the money back into his team. Tony Morley arrived for £200,000, David Geddis for a club record £300,000, and the following season centre-forward Peter Withe for another record £500,000.

Withe – tall, powerful, aggressive and with an eye for a goal – proved to be the final piece of a jigsaw that would give Villa a perfectly balanced team. His 20 goals in the 1980–81 season, alongside Gary Shaw's 18, provided the spearhead to bring the First Division title back to Villa Park for the first time since 1910.

The triumph brought a European adventure which started with a trip to Iceland to face FC Valur and ended one heady night in Rotterdam the following May when Withe's goal, stabbed home from a few yards from Morley's cross, saw the club beat mighty Bayern Munich to be crowned as European champions.

Saunders, however, was no longer in charge. He had fallen out with the club's directors as intrigue behind the scenes took hold and resigned his post in February – causing sensation by taking over as manager at Birmingham a few days later. Assistant Tony Barton stepped up to take temporary charge, did well, and ended up as the man who will always be remembered as the manager of Aston Villa's European Cup-winning team.

The Blues' decision to appoint Saunders caused controversy

on both sides of the city. After suffering relegation, Jim Smith had brought the club back to the First Division at the first attempt and achieved a respectable mid-table finish. The new manager changed the emphasis at Birmingham from the flamboyant attacking football which Smith had loved to a more functional style – but the St Andrew's crowd loved the passion of figures like Robert Hopkins, Mick Harford and Mick Dennis who fought with pride for the club they represented.

Life at Birmingham in the 1980s became a bit of a rollercoaster, however. Relegated again in 1984, they stuck with Saunders to bring them back at the first attempt – but a tragedy on the final day of the 1984–85 season had dramatic consequences. Fans of Leeds and Birmingham rioted, and in the confusion a wall collapsed, killing a young supporter. The official enquiry that followed ordered a number of fences and other stadium safety measures, and the cost of that work impacted on the team. It also hastened a change of ownership that saw savage cost-cutting measures brought in. Relegated under John Bond in 1986 after losing a club record 29 League games in one season, by 1989 Birmingham had gone down again. The scale of the crisis was shown up by a crowd of just 4,026 to see a League game against Swindon – the lowest gate since 1913.

Villa had problems of their own, meanwhile, as the 1980s became another big let-down. They followed up their European Cup glory by also winning the European Super Cup. But when Doug Ellis resumed as chairman in the face of massive financial problems, his attempts to cut costs impacted on the playing squad. He sacked Tony Barton and brought in Graham Turner from Shrewsbury with instructions to break up the European Cup team and bring through younger players. It ended badly as Turner was sacked and his replacement Billy McNeill couldn't stop Villa from being relegated in 1987. Just five years after being crowned kings of Europe, they were back in the Second Division.

It proved a turning point. While at Birmingham things were going from bad to worse, Villa's new manager Graham Taylor mounted a promotion campaign with new heroes whose names are still sung by the Holte End – Nigel Spink, Paul Birch and Alan McInally. And he followed that by almost winning the First Division title, ending the 1989–90 season as runners-up – a feat which earned him the invitation to take over as manager of England.

Record in the 1980s

Aston Villa:

Season	League	P	W	D	L	F	A	Pts	Position
1980–81	Div 1	42	26	8	8	72	40	60	1
1981–82	Div 1	42	15	12	15	55	53	57*	11
1982–83	Div 1	42	21	5	16	62	50	68	6
1983–84	Div 1	42	17	9	16	59	61	60	10
1984–85	Div 1	42	15	11	16	60	60	56	10
1985–86	Div 1	42	10	14	18	51	67	44	16
1986–87	Div 1	42	8	12	22	45	79	36	22
1987–88	Div 2	44	22	12	10	68	41	78	2
1988–89	Div 1	38	9	13	16	45	56	40	17
1989–90	Div 1	38	21	7	10	57	38	70	2

*1981–82 was the start of three points for a win.

FA Cup

1980–81	0-1 v Ipswich Town (third round)
1981–82	0-1 v Tottenham Hotspur (fifth round)
1982–83	0-2 v Arsenal (sixth round)
1983–84	1-1, 0-3 v Norwich City (third round)
1984–85	0-3 v Liverpool (third round)
1985–86	1-1, 0-1 v Millwall (fourth round)
1986–87	2-2, 1-2 v Chelsea (third round)
1987–88	0-2 v Liverpool (fourth round)

| 1988–89 | 0-1 v Wimbledon (fourth round) |
| 1989–90 | 0-3 v Oldham Athletic (sixth round) |

Football League Cup

1980–81	1-2 v Cambridge United (third round)
1981–82	0-1 v West Bromwich Albion (fifth round)
1982–83	1-2, 0-1 v Notts County (second round, over two legs)
1983–84	0-2, 1-0 v Everton (semi-final, over two legs)
1984–85	0-1 v Queens Park Rangers (third round)
1985–86	2-2, 1-2 v Oxford United (semi-final, over two legs)
1986–87	1-2 v Southampton (fourth round)
1987–88	1-2 v Sheffield Wednesday (fourth round)
1988–89	1-2 v West Ham United (fifth round)
1989–90	0-0, 0-1 v West Ham United (third round)

European Competition

1980–81	did not qualify
1981–82	European Cup Winners 1-0 v Bayern Munich (final in Rotterdam)
1982–83	European Cup 1-2, 1-3 v Juventus (third round)
1983–84	UEFA Cup 2-2, 1-2 v Spartak Moscow (second round)
1984–85	did not qualify
1985–86	did not qualify
1986–87	did not qualify
1987–88	did not qualify
1988–89	did not qualify
1989–90	did not qualify

Birmingham:

Season	League	P	W	D	L	F	A	Pts	Position
1980–81	Div 1	42	13	12	17	50	61	38	13
1981–82	Div 1	42	10	14	18	53	61	44*	16
1982–83	Div 1	42	12	14	16	40	55	50	17

1983–84	Div 1	42	12	12	18	39	50	48	20
1984–85	Div 2	42	25	7	10	59	33	82	2
1985–86	Div 1	42	8	5	29	30	73	29	21
1986–87	Div 2	42	11	17	14	47	59	50	19
1987–88	Div 2	44	11	15	18	41	66	48	19
1988–89	Div 2	46	8	11	27	31	76	35	23
1989–90	Div 3	46	18	12	16	60	59	66	7

*1981–82 was the start of three points for a win.

FA Cup

1980–81	2-3 v Coventry City (fourth round)
1981–82	2-3 v Ipswich Town (third round)
1982–83	0-1 v Crystal Palace (fourth round)
1983–84	1-3 v Watford (sixth round)
1984–85	0-0, 1-1, 1-1, 0-1 v Norwich (third round)
1985–86	1-2 v Altrincham (third round)
1986–87	0-1 v Walsall (fourth round)
1987–88	0-1 v Nottingham Forest (fifth round)
1988–89	0-1 v Wimbledon (third round)
1989–90	1-1, 0-1 v Oldham Athletic (third round)

Football League Cup

1980–81	1-3 v Liverpool (fifth round)
1981–82	3-3, 1-2 v Nottingham Forest (second round, over two legs)
1982–83	2-3 v Burnley (fourth round)
1983–84	1-1, 0-3 v Liverpool (semi-final, over two legs)
1984–85	0-0, 1-3 v West Bromwich Albion (third round)
1985–86	1-1, 0-3 v Southampton (third round)
1986–87	0-5 v Tottenham Hotspur (third round)
1987–88	2-2, 0-1 v Mansfield Town (first round)
1988–89	0-2, 0-5 v Aston Villa (second round, over two legs)
1989–90	1-2, 1-1 v West Ham (second round, over two legs)

11th October 1980

Division One
Birmingham 1
Worthington (pen)
Aston Villa 2
Cowans (pen), Evans
Attendance: **33,879**
BIRMINGHAM: *Wealands, Langan, Dennis, Curbishley, Gallagher, Todd, Ainscow, Lynex, Worthington, Gemmill, Dillon*
ASTON VILLA: *Rimmer, Swain, Deacy, Evans, McNaught, Mortimer, Bremner, Shaw, Withe, Cowans, Morley*

Ron Saunders had based much of his work in his six seasons at Villa Park on team spirit and togetherness, and this was to be the campaign that saw those virtues achieve their ultimate domestic prize.

Villa ended the campaign as First Division champions, some 71 years since the club had last been England's top team.

But what was more remarkable was that Saunders' side achieved the feat with a squad of just 14 players, of whom seven played in every single match.

That togetherness enabled them to chip victories out of tight matches – a virtue proved in the hostile atmosphere of St Andrew's.

The winning goal came just six minutes from time, scored by defender Allan Evans when he went forward for a free-kick.

His fellow defender Ken McNaught hoisted the ball into the box and Evans, who had been a centre-forward when he first moved to Villa from Scotland, showed a striker's instincts as he turned and made space for himself before rifling home a tremendous drive.

Evans had been forced to be on top form early in the game as the Blues dominated – while McNaught saved a certain goal as he managed to deny Frank Worthington by acrobatically clearing the ball with an overhead kick on the goal-line.

Villa went in front through a disputed penalty when Mark Dennis was ruled to have handled – Gordon Cowans was completely calm as he waited for the protests to die down before slotting the kick beyond the reach of Geoff Wealands.

There were more arguments to come when the Blues drew level, again from the spot. Alan Ainscow was held up as he tried to wriggle between McNaught and Eamonn Deacy – this time Worthington showed patience to let the arguments stop before scoring.

It began to look as if both teams would have to settle for a point, but then came the late winner.

13th December 1980

Division One

Aston Villa 3

Geddis (2), Shaw

Birmingham 0

Attendance: 41,101

ASTON VILLA: *Rimmer, Swain, Williams, Evans, McNaught, Mortimer, Bremner, Shaw, Geddis, Cowans, Morley*

BIRMINGHAM: *Wealands, Langan, Hawker, Curbishley (Lynex), Gallagher, Todd, Ainscow, Bertschin, Worthington, Gemmill, Dillon*

Villa's early-season form, including a run of nine wins and two draws in 11 games, had swept them to the top of the First Division table – but they then hit a run of four without a win and nerves were starting to become frayed on derby day.

Jim Smith's team had won promotion thanks to the inspired signing half way through the campaign of great entertainer Frank Worthington, and the unpredictable forward was enjoying one of the best spells of his career after getting back to the top flight.

Neither side created much in a tight first half, in which Dennis Mortimer was struggling to find space to give winger Tony Morley any possession to run at Birmingham's defence.

Alan Curbishley and Kevin Dillon combined well to play some attractive passing football for the Blues, although they lacked any real penetration to supply chances for Worthington.

With 64 minutes gone David Geddis, playing because Peter Withe was suspended, burst into the game to open the scoring and begin a 20-minute assault which left the Blues battered.

He got another himself before hitting the post with a shot which enabled Gary Shaw to follow up with a tap-in to settle an emphatic victory.

Geddis, signed the previous season for a club record £300,000, had scored on his only previous appearance during the season and was anxious to prove a point about his lack of first-team opportunities.

He said: "I know that even if I'd scored a hat-trick I wouldn't feel I would keep my place once Peter returns from suspension but I do feel I am a thorn in the manager's side.

"The display gives me a lot of confidence. I am very much in the shop window and perhaps I have sold myself to somebody."

26th September 1981

Division One
Aston Villa 0
Birmingham 0
Attendance: 41,098
ASTON VILLA: *Rimmer, Swain, Gibson, Evans, Ormsby, Mortimer, Bremner, Blair, Withe, Cowans, Morley*
BIRMINGHAM: *Wealands, Langan, Dennis, Dillon, Broadhurst, Todd, Brocken (Handysides), Whatmore, Worthington, Gemmill, Van Mierlo*

Defending Football League champions Villa made a poor start to the new season with only one win in six games by the time they faced Blues.

Ron Saunders had made just one signing in the summer to

strengthen his squad, paying Coventry £350,000 for Andy Blair.

The midfielder had been forced to wait for his debut, but with Gary Shaw and Terry Donovan both injured he was brought into the starting side for the first time.

Blues had their flamboyant forward Frank Worthington back for his first full match since spending the summer playing in the United States.

Torrential rain pounded the Birmingham area all night and during the morning – giving a test for Villa's revolutionary new plastic pitch cover which was left in place until an hour before kick-off, by which time the groundstaff had removed half a million gallons of water from it.

It was a tense and aggressive match, with Archie Gemmill needing treatment twice in the early stages after heavy tackles from Villa defender Allan Evans.

Peter Withe was booked for a heavy tackle on Kevan Broadhurst, as the two tussled with each other throughout the match, while Colin Todd was booked in the second half for hacking down Blair on the one occasion the new boy threatened to break free.

Villa's injuries meant they had a patched-up front line. Withe was the only recognized forward and the plan was for Gordon Cowans and Blair to get up alongside him but it didn't really work.

It was Villa keeper Jimmy Rimmer who had to make the most significant save, keeping out Kevin Dillon's shot. City also claimed in vain that they should have had a penalty when Worthington was brought down.

20ᵗʰ February 1982

Division One
Birmingham 0
Aston Villa 1
Withe
Attendance: **32,817**
BIRMINGHAM: *Jones, Langan, Van Den Hauwe, Curbishley, Scott, Broadhurst, Handysides, Whatmore, Worthington, Phillips, Van Mierlo*
ASTON VILLA: *Rimmer, Swain (Bullivant), Williams, Evans, McNaught, Mortimer, Bremner, Shaw, Withe, Cowans, Morley*

Fate and the fixture list turned this into the "Ron Saunders derby". Days after losing his job as manager of Aston Villa following a series of fall-outs with chairman Doug Ellis, the man who had won the First Division title the previous season accepted an offer to become manager of their most deadly rivals.

With a quirk of fortune that couldn't have been scripted, his very first match in charge was at home to Villa.

Saunders did his best to keep a low profile during the game, taking a seat in the directors' box alongside vice-chairman Jack Wiseman.

Birmingham fans weren't happy at the dismissal of Jim Smith that had brought the change – and comedian Jasper Carrott resigned from his position of director in protest that he had not been consulted.

Before going into the ground he told reporters: "My resignation was over a matter of principle. I don't know how I would have voted, but I would have welcomed the chance to sit down and thrash the matter out."

The background of boardroom drama added spice to the atmosphere. Police had to break up a couple of fights on the terraces, while on the pitch Villa full-back Ken Swain was hurt in a first-minute tackle and had to go off shortly afterwards.

Villa still looked the better team, and Allan Evans hit the bar with a header from a Gordon Cowans free-kick.

Cowans was dictating the game, hitting good passes to give winger Tony Morley the opportunity to run at Birmingham's defence.

And it was Morley who set up the only goal, swinging over a cross that defender Geoff Scott misjudged leaving Peter Withe the simple chance to prod the ball home.

27th December 1982

Division One

Birmingham 3
Blake, Handysides, Ferguson

Aston Villa 0

Attendance: 43,864

BIRMINGHAM: *Coton, Langan, Van Den Hauwe, Stevenson, Blake, Broadhurst, Dillon, Harford, Ferguson, Curbishley, Handysides*

ASTON VILLA: *Rimmer, Jones, Williams, Evans, McNaught, Mortimer, Bremner, Shaw, Withe, Cowans, Walters*

Villa had turned the city claret and blue by winning the European Cup in May and would go on to beat Barcelona over two legs to add the European Super Cup to their silverware.

But all of that prestige went out of the window when it came to a good old-fashioned "battle of Brum" and if anything was all the more incentive for Birmingham to come up with their best performance in a St Andrew's derby since 1968.

Ron Saunders had taken the club through a massive shake-up since taking charge 10 months earlier, going back to Aston Villa to sign giant young defender Noel Blake as the cornerstone of his defence.

The 20-year-old, born and brought up in Jamaica but found by Villa playing non-League football with Sutton Coldfield, relished the chance to show his old club what he might have done for them.

He won a hugely physical battle to keep experienced centre-forward Peter Withe out of the game – and topped his man-of-the-match performance off by scoring the first goal.

Just for good measure he showed his courage by insisting he would play on after being struck by a coin thrown from the crowd early in the second half, with referee Ray Lewis having to stop the game for nearly three minutes while he was treated.

Blake's goal came after 22 minutes, a calm sidefoot after an Ian Handysides shot had beaten Jimmy Rimmer but rebounded off the post into his path.

Though Villa had much of the play for a while afterwards, their attack carried little threat and it was Handysides who put the Blues further in front with 69 minutes gone, following up to tap home the rebound after Rimmer had failed to hold his shot.

Mike Ferguson added the third to clinch a result that lifted Birmingham off the foot of the First Division table – it took a last-minute clearance by Gary Williams to stop Handysides making the scoreline even more emphatic.

It was inevitably another physical battle, with Allan Evans and Mark Walters of Villa joining Birmingham's Kevin Dillon, David Langan and Pat Van Den Hauwe in the referee's notebook.

4ᵗʰ April 1983

Division One

Aston Villa 1

Shaw

Birmingham 0

Attendance: 40,897

ASTON VILLA: *Spink, Williams, Gibson, Evans, McNaught, Mortimer, Bremner (Curbishley), Shaw, Withe, Cowans, Walters*

BIRMINGHAM: *Coton, Hagan, Dennis, Stevenson, Blake, Van Den Hauwe, Gayle, Ferguson, Harford, Halsall, Hopkins*

While a good number of players have moved from Aston Villa to Birmingham at different times, very few have moved in the opposite direction – but Alan Curbishley was one exception to the rule.

The midfielder hadn't fitted too comfortably into the work ethic of Birmingham's team, but Villa boss Tony Barton felt his passing ability made him a perfect addition to a side who were still the reigning European champions, even if their hopes of retaining their title had been ended in a controversial defeat to Italian side Juventus.

Curbishley made his debut as a second-half substitute in this game, having arrived at Villa Park in a part-exchange deal that saw tenacious young winger Robert Hopkins move the other way.

Hopkins, brought up as a passionate Blues fan, had made his debut immediately and was already on the way to becoming a cult hero of the terraces for his fully committed performances.

After losing so heavily at Christmas, however, Barton made sure that his Villa team were charged up for the return match and they defended superbly in a tight game, with centre-half Ken McNaught impressive against Mick Harford.

Harford did manage to break free of his attentions on a couple of occasions, though, only to miss good opportunities – especially after Howard Gayle had run through Villa's defence.

The Blues were punished when 10 minutes after half-time Gary Shaw scored, running on to the ball to finish instinctively after Peter Withe had glanced on a long clearance by goalkeeper Nigel Spink.

It was Villa's seventh win in 10 League games, and left Barton promising they would finish high enough to qualify for the following season's UEFA Cup – he was proved right.

Birmingham boss Ron Saunders took solace from a battling performance by a much-changed team – only two of his starting line-up had played for the club on the opening day of the season.

"We came here as the sacrificial lambs and we did very well," was his verdict. "We showed an abundance of determination and I have no doubt if we continue like that we will get away from relegation trouble."

He was also proved right – City won five of their last six games to finish comfortably safe.

15th October 1983

Division One
Aston Villa 1
Withe
Birmingham 0
Attendance: 39,318
ASTON VILLA: *Spink, Williams, Gibson, Evans, Ormsby, Mortimer, Curbishley, Walters, Withe, McMahon, Morley (Bremner)*
BIRMINGHAM: *Coton, Hagan, Van Den Hauwe, Blake, Wright, Broadhurst (Stevenson), Gayle, Rees, Harford, Halsall, Hopkins*

Maybe it was the torrential rain that left puddles all over the pitch. Maybe it was that both sets of players were still carrying grudges from their previous bad-tempered encounter.

Whatever the reason, this was one of the most spiteful of contests in the hundred-year history of meetings between the two second city rivals.

The feuds started with City centre-forward Mick Harford catching Villa skipper Allan Evans with a late challenge the first time they competed for the ball, and didn't stop until the final whistle and beyond.

Full-back Jim Hagan needed extensive treatment after clashing with Tony Morley as they both competed for a long clearance by Brendan Ormsby.

But the clash which really ignited tempers was when Robert Hopkins caught Mark Walters in an off-the-ball incident.

Peter Withe and Allan Evans both stormed into a group of players to remonstrate with their former club-mate Hopkins, and the player was pulled away by Noel Blake.

It was typical of the game that the only goal, scored after 20 minutes, was a scrappy affair. Withe gambled by chasing Pat Van Den Hauwe's backpass and got lucky when the ball stuck in a puddle, enabling him to push it round goalkeeper Tony Coton and roll it to the empty net.

Blake claimed he had equalized, insisting the ball had crossed the line after his header had hit the inside of the post and been clawed away by goalkeeper Nigel Spink.

But there were greater controversies to come. With 61 minutes gone Colin Gibson brought down Howard Gayle as the Blues winger sprinted clear and was sent off despite heated protests.

Birmingham skipper Kevan Broadhurst had to go off after being caught in a ferocious tackle from Steve McMahon which might have merited greater punishment than a booking.

The Blues had a penalty awarded for hand ball, from which Spink brilliantly kept out Blake's spot-kick.

After the final whistle McMahon and Blake clashed in the centre circle – and as they exchanged words the Birmingham centre-half aimed a head-butt at Villa's midfield man.

31st March 1984

Division One
Birmingham 2
Stevenson, Gayle
Aston Villa 1
Withe
Attendance: 23,993
BIRMINGHAM: *Coton, Roberts, Hagan, Blake, Kuhl, Stevenson, Gayle, Van Den Hauwe, McCarrick, Halsall, Hopkins*
ASTON VILLA: *Day, Williams, Gibson (Bremner), Evans, Ormsby, Curbishley, Birch, Walters, Withe, McMahon, Rideout*

After the bitter fall-out from the Villa Park meeting, the Football League put referee John Hunting, the man chosen to take charge of this season's FA Cup final, in charge for the return.

Both teams talked about avoiding the excesses of the first contest, but there were less than 60 seconds gone when Robert Hopkins crashed into a tackle on Colin Gibson.

Hopkins escaped with a warning from the ref, but the damage was already done, with Gibson having to go off injured and be replaced by substitute Des Bremner.

Mr Hunting's decision to keep his notebook in his pocket and deal with incidents by talking to the players seemed to work, however, and both teams began to concentrate on playing football.

Mark Walters volleyed just over at one end after Peter Withe had chested the ball cleverly into his path, then at the other Mervyn Day threw himself bravely at the feet of Howard Gayle after Allan Evans had slipped to give the winger a clear run at goal.

Villa failed to clear the corner that followed, and as the ball bobbled on the edge of the box Byron Stevenson turned to hook it over Day's head and into the top corner.

Villa's response was first-class. Tony Coton had to keep out an Evans shot after Paul Birch headed on a Walters centre, and then saved a fierce drive by Steve McMahon.

But almost inevitably the equalizer came through Peter Withe, arriving unmarked at the back post for a simple header after Alan Curbishley's quick thinking at a throw-in gave Paul Rideout space to hit the cross.

Withe had another chance just before the break – but 36 seconds after the restart Gayle got behind the defence to collect Stevenson's clearance, and ran from 20 yards inside Villa's half to score a fine individual goal.

Villa claimed that Rideout's header with 20 minutes left had crossed the line before Tony Coton could claw it away, and wanted a penalty for hand ball – but this was Birmingham's day. Sadly, however, it proved to be their last win of the season and they were relegated.

7th September 1985

Division One

Birmingham 0

Aston Villa 0

Attendance: 24,971

BIRMINGHAM: *Seaman, Roberts, Jones, Wright, Armstrong, Kuhl, Dicks, Clarke, Kennedy, Geddis, Hopkins*

ASTON VILLA: *Spink, Williams, Dorigo, Evans, Ormsby, Bradley (Walker), Birch, Walters, Gray, Hodge, Daley*

After winning promotion at the first attempt, Ron Saunders' team made a solid start to the new season and saw the derby as the chance for a huge morale boost.

The result was another feisty affair with Robert Hopkins again the centre of controversy for a challenge on Darren Bradley which left Villa's young midfielder unable to finish the game.

Goalkeeper Nigel Spink was booked for complaining to referee Norman Wilson about the incident as tempers again threatened to boil over.

The Blues gave a debut to teenager Julian Dicks after Des Bremner, transferred from Villa a year earlier to be a key part of the promotion-winning team, failed a fitness test.

The home team showed their intentions by forcing two corners in the first five minutes, and there were signs of nerves from Villa new boy Steve Hodge who had recently signed from Nottingham Forest in a £400,000 move.

Spink made a couple of mistakes, but was rescued by the experience of defender Allan Evans who cleared off the line from David Geddis – and just before half-time it took another dramatic goal-line clearance by Tony Dorigo to stop the same player from breaking the deadlock.

But Villa battled gamely, and the nearest they came to conceding in the second half was when Brendan Orsmby blocked an overhead kick from Andy Kennedy using his arm, though the referee ruled it to be accidental – and then with four minutes left a thunderous shot from debut boy Dicks brought a brilliant save from Spink.

Villa manager Graham Turner found positives, claiming: "Not so long ago the team would have buckled under the pressure. You have to learn to weather storms like this in order to put a run of results together."

22nd March 1986

Division One
Aston Villa 0
Birmingham 3
Clarke (2), Whitton
Attendance: **26,894**
ASTON VILLA: *Spink, Williams, Dorigo, Evans, Elliott, Hunt, Blair, Shaw, Gray, Hodge, Walters*
BIRMINGHAM: *Seaman, Ranson, Roberts, Hagan, Garton, Kuhl, Bremner, Clarke, Wright, Whitton, Hopkins*

The early-season optimism at St Andrew's had long since dissolved and Birmingham were a club facing massive problems both on and off the field.

Financial restrictions made it impossible for Ron Saunders to strengthen the team he had brought back to the top flight, and a desperate run of just two draws in 17 League matches, plus an FA Cup exit at home to non-League Altrincham, saw him lose his job in January.

New manager John Bond signed centre-forward Steve Whitton which gave some brief impetus, but by the time his team headed to Villa Park they had lost another three games in a row.

But the nerves of being expected to win a big game got to Villa's young team and they handed victory on a plate to their visitors.

City had not scored a goal at Villa Park for nine years, but with

31 minutes gone, defender Paul Elliott misjudged a long clearance by goalkeeper David Seaman to present Wayne Clarke with the easiest of chances.

Seven minutes later Des Bremner harried Allan Evans into an error to give Clarke his second goal.

The match was something of a personal triumph for Bremner, part of Villa's European Cup-winning side but discarded two years earlier by manager Graham Turner as too old to fit in his plans.

He gave Steve Hunt no room in midfield as the Blues bossed the game. The third goal after 62 minutes was yet another defensive disaster, with Nigel Spink caught in two minds over whether to come for Ray Ranson's long clearance to give Whitton an easy opportunity.

It gave Bond brief hope of working a miracle at the foot of the table, and his side drew 1-1 with Manchester United a week later. But another dismal run losing every one of their last seven games, and scoring only one goal in the process, left them doomed to the drop again.

22nd August 1987

Division Two

Aston Villa 0

Birmingham 2

Rees, Handysides

Attendance: 30,870

ASTON VILLA: *Spink, Gage, Gallacher, Cooper, Sims, Keown, Birch, Aspinall, Stainrod (Daley), D. Hunt (S. Hunt), Walters*

BIRMINGHAM: *Godden, Roberts, Dicks, Williams, Overson, Handysides, Bremner, Kennedy, Whitton, Rees, Wigley*

Thunder and lightning rolled around Villa Park on derby day, which was pretty apt as both clubs were going through stormy times.

Villa had followed Birmingham into the Second Division and chairman Doug Ellis turned to Watford manager Graham Taylor to rescue the club.

He started work to rebuild the side – but on a limited budget – paying £50,000 for defender Steve Sims from his old club and getting midfielder David Hunt on a free transfer.

This result – and performance – helped him convince his board that he needed more backing to strengthen the side further.

Meanwhile the Blues were going through bad times of their own, with manager Garry Pendrey recruited by new owner Ken Wheldon who was savagely cutting costs at the club.

Pendrey, as a player the youngest to captain the club, knew the importance to the fans of a derby clash in the second game of the season and brought a great performance from his limited team.

It was a dour battle, with 24 free-kicks awarded for fouls in the first half, and a couple of runs by Villa's Mark Walters were about the only sign of creativity.

It was typical of the performance, however, that when he dribbled practically the length of the field he then failed to pick out either Paul Birch or Simon Stainrod who were both unmarked.

Six minutes after half-time City were far more clinical. Sims failed to get any distance on his header as he defended a corner, and Tony Rees hooked the ball back beyond the reach of Nigel Spink.

The second was a superb effort. Steve Whitton held the ball up well and fed it to Ian Handysides, who struck a brilliant 25-yard shot that gave Spink no chance.

12th December 1987

Division Two

Birmingham 1

Kennedy

Aston Villa 2

Thompson (2)

Attendance: 27,789

BIRMINGHAM: *Godden, Ranson, Trewick, Roberts, Overson, Frain (Russell), Bremner, Childs, Kennedy, Handysides, Wigley*

ASTON VILLA: *Spink, Gage, Gallacher, Lillis, Sims, Keown, Birch, Aspinall, Thompson, S. Gray, Walters*

Both teams walked out side-by-side as a gesture of cordiality – but all that was forgotten as soon as the match started.

City defender Ray Ranson ploughed into a bad foul on Stuart Gray, while Villa centre-forward Garry Thompson seemed to be constantly squabbling with Vince Overson and several other feuds developed around the pitch.

The conflict spilled to the terraces, with police rushing to keep apart Villa fans who were overspilling from the Tilton Road End and being taunted by their opposite numbers on the Kop.

Thankfully attention was brought back to the pitch when with 13 minutes gone Kevin Gage swung over a cross that was met by a superb diving header from Garry Thompson – his fifth headed goal in four matches since recovering from an injury which had kept him out for the first part of the season.

Birmingham hit back through Andy Kennedy, latching on to a clever left-foot cross by Gary Childs to drag the ball wide of Nigel Spink and roll it to the inviting net.

There was more trouble in the crowd at half-time, and play was held up for a couple of minutes when one supporter ran onto the pitch.

That seemed to break Birmingham's concentration, and Villa cashed in with an almost identical goal to the first as Thompson dived to meet another Gage cross.

Kennedy had a couple of half-chances as the Blues looked for an equalizer, but it was home keeper Tony Godden who made the best save to keep out a late effort from Mark Walters.

It proved a crucial stage in Villa's season as Thompson's impact at centre-forward – he scored 11 goals in 24 games – saw them clinch a return to the First Division.

27th September 1988

Football League Cup – Second Round

First Leg

Birmingham 0

Aston Villa 2

Gage, Gray

Attendance: 21,177

ASTON VILLA: *Spink, Price, Mountfield, A. Gray, Gage, Keown, Daley, Platt, Thompson, Cowans, Gallacher*

BIRMINGHAM: *Godden, Ranson (Bremner), Roberts, Atkins, Overson, Clarkson, Morris, Langley, Yates, Robinson (Whitton), Wigley*

Birmingham's reward for beating Wolves across two legs in the first round of the League Cup was an even more prestigious local derby.

It was the first time the clubs had been drawn together in a major Cup competition for 26 seasons – ironically they would also meet later that autumn in the newly created Simod Cup.

Blues boss Garry Pendrey took the chance to give experience to some of his youngsters, picking 17-year-old Ian Clarkson for his debut in a side that also included 18-year-old strikers Ronnie Morris and Mark Yates.

Morris gave a promising performance, inspiring most of his team's best attacking moves throughout the game as Nigel Spink had to make saves from both Yates and Steve Wigley.

But Birmingham's defensive frailties were all too obvious. With six minutes gone Andy Gray (recruited in the summer from Crystal Palace and not to be confused with the hero centre-forward of a decade earlier) took a corner on the right. It was headed down by Garry Thompson to where Kevin Gage, with his back to goal, swivelled to put a shot beyond the reach of Tony Godden.

Just before half-time David Platt managed to gain possession from a Tony Daley cross, and held the ball long enough to give Gordon Cowans the chance to start another move which ended with Gray hitting a 20-yard shot. Birmingham fought back well, and Villa manager Graham Taylor kept his side in the dressing room afterwards to demand more from them.

He said: "I was hoping after half-time we would put the tie beyond them, but our second-half display was the worst we have played this season."

12th October 1988

Football League Cup – Second Round
Second Leg
Aston Villa 5
Mountfield, Gage (2), Olney, Daley
Birmingham 0
Attendance: 19,753
ASTON VILLA: *Spink, Price, Mountfield, Evans, Gage, Sims, Daley, Platt, Olney, Cowans, S. Gray (Gallacher)*
BIRMINGHAM: *Elliott, Ranson (Sturridge), Frain, Atkins, Overson, Clarkson, Bremner, Peer, Morris (Childs), Robinson, Wigley*

There was torrential rain for the second leg, and a torrent of goals too as Villa heeded their manager's call to be more ruthless.

After the successful experiment with some of his youngsters in the match at St Andrew's, Garry Pendrey chose to give 18-year-old goalkeeper Tony Elliott, a former England Youth international, his debut.

That decision didn't turn out so well, however, and the youngster was at fault on a couple of occasions as Villa scored four goals in 17 minutes in the first half.

He couldn't be blamed for the opening strike which took just 45 seconds. Derek Mountfield's powerful header from a Gordon Cowans corner on the left gave him no chance.

But 10 minutes later he fumbled a harmless-looking free-kick from Kevin Gage and spilled the ball over the line.

Gage scored again with a 25-yard volley from a Cowans free-kick, and a minute after that poor Elliott allowed Ian Olney's shot to squirm under his body.

Villa had brought the experience of Steve Sims and Allan Evans back into their team and the difference in class told – although they took their foot off the pedal after half-time.

But with so much possession another goal was certain to come, and Tony Daley's 20-yard shot completed a comprehensive victory.

It turned out to be the only game that Elliott, highly rated having come through the FA's Academy school at Lilleshall, ever played for the club. He moved on to Hereford shortly afterwards, but had a successful career playing nearly 200 League games and now runs coaching clinics.

Villa, incidentally, went even better when the teams met in the Simod Cup in November, coming out 6-0 winners thanks to two goals from Alan McInally and others by David Platt, Bernard Gallacher, Derek Mountfield and Allan Evans.

Chapter Nine

The 1990s

Graham Taylor's departure to become England manager left Doug Ellis in search of his sixth manager in the nine years since he had returned to take over the running of the club – and he caused surprise by choosing an unexpected route.

Nowadays top clubs all look across the world before they choose managerial candidates, even if they end up making an appointment from Britain. Back in 1990 Aston Villa's chairman was breaking new ground when he named Czech national coach Dr Josef Vengloš as Taylor's successor.

As runners-up the previous season Villa were leading the way, together with Manchester United, to return to European competition after the ban on English clubs playing in Europe which had lasted five years. A quirk of fate in the UEFA Cup draw paired them with the doctor's old Czech club Banik Ostrava. After successfully negotiating that round there followed a thrilling 2-0 home leg win over Inter Milan, only to lose 3-0 in the San Siro and go out.

Sadly the win over Milan proved all too brief an adventure in a season that went steadily downhill as the experiment with different Continental thinking failed. Villa just avoided relegation – and Dr Vengloš was dismissed to make way for former Manchester United manager Ron Atkinson.

His arrival sparked a dramatic transformation. By the time the newly formed Premier League began in 1992, Villa had a side of dash and flair with the goalscoring prowess of Dean Saunders and Dalian Atkinson at its cutting edge and they went head-to-head with Manchester United in a thrilling race for the inaugural Premier

League title, ultimately stumbling in the last few weeks.

The next season at least brought partial revenge with a Wembley victory over United in the League Cup. It set the tone for an exciting decade. Atkinson was sacked after a poor start the following season, but his successor Brian Little took the team back to Wembley to win the League Cup in 1996 by beating Leeds and also reached the FA Cup semi-final, as well as qualifying for Europe in each of the next three seasons.

Across the city the 1990s began at an all-time low at St Andrew's. Manager Terry Cooper earned promotion back to the second tier, but then had to steer the club through being placed into administration as the recession caused the collapse of the clothing empire of owners the Kumar brothers. Salvation came when multi-millionaire David Sullivan bought Birmingham from the receiver and controversially installed 24-year-old Karren Brady as his managing director.

The Blues were relegated again under Barry Fry, but new investment turned the tide. A Wembley win in the 1995 Auto Windscreens Shield lifted spirits, the club won promotion back to the second tier – and when former golden boy Trevor Francis came back to St Andrew's as manager they began to fight for a place in the Premier League, although missed out three times in the play-offs.

Record in the 1990s

Aston Villa:

Season	League	P	W	D	L	F	A	Pts	Position
1990–91	Div 1	38	9	14	15	46	58	41	17
1991–92	Div 1	42	17	9	16	48	44	60	7
1992–93	Premier	42	21	11	10	57	40	74	2
1993–94	Premier	42	15	12	15	46	50	57	10
1994–95	Premier	42	11	15	16	51	56	48	18

1995–96	Premier 38	18	9	11	52	35	63	4
1996–97	Premier 38	17	10	11	47	34	61	5
1997–98	Premier 38	17	6	15	49	48	57	7
1998–99	Premier 38	15	10	13	51	46	55	6
1999-2000	Premier 38	15	13	10	46	35	58	6

FA Cup

1990–91	1-1, 0-1 v Wimbledon (third round)
1991–92	0-1 v Liverpool (sixth round)
1992–93	1-1, 0-1 v Wimbledon (fourth round)
1993–94	0-1 v Bolton Wanderers (fifth round)
1994–95	0-1 v Manchester City (fourth round)
1995–96	0-3 v Liverpool (semi-final)
1996–97	1-3 v Derby County (fourth round)
1997–98	0-1 v Coventry City (fifth round)
1998–99	0-2 v Fulham (fourth round)
1999-2000	0-1 v Chelsea (final at Wembley Stadium)

Football League Cup

1990–91	1-4 v Leeds United (fifth round)
1991–92	0-0, 1-1 v Grimsby Town (second round, over two legs, lost on away goal)
1992–93	2-2, 0-1 v Ipswich Town (fourth round)
1993–94	3-1 v Manchester United (final at Wembley Stadium)
1994–95	1-4 v Crystal Palace (fourth round)
1995–96	3-0 v Leeds United (final at Wembley Stadium)
1996–97	0-1 v Wimbledon (fourth round)
1997–98	0-3 v West Ham United (third round)
1998–99	1-4 v Chelsea (third round)
1999-2000	0-0, 0-1 v Leicester City (semi-final, over two legs)

European Competition

| 1990–91 | UEFA Cup 2-0, 0-3 v Inter Milan (second round) |

1991–92	did not qualify
1992–93	did not qualify
1993–94	UEFA Cup 1-1, 0-1 v Deportivo La Coruña (second round)
1994–95	UEFA Cup 0-1, 2-1 v Trabzonspor (second round)
1995–96	did not qualify
1996–97	UEFA Cup 1-1, 0-0 v Helsingborgs IF (first round, lost on away goal)
1997–98	UEFA Cup 0-1, 2-1 v Atlético Madrid (fourth round)
1998–99	UEFA Cup 1-0, 1-3 v Celta Vigo (second round)
1999–2000	did not qualify

Birmingham:

Season	League	P	W	D	L	F	A	Pts	Position
1990–91	Div 3	46	16	17	13	45	49	65	12
1991–92	Div 3	46	23	12	11	69	52	81	2
*1992–93	Tier 2	46	13	12	21	50	72	51	19
1993–94	Tier 2	46	13	12	21	52	69	51	22
1994–95	Tier 3	46	25	14	7	84	37	89	1
1995–96	Tier 2	46	15	13	18	61	64	58	15
1996–97	Tier 2	46	17	15	14	52	48	66	10
1997–98	Tier 2	46	19	17	10	60	35	74	7
1998–99	Tier 2	46	23	12	11	66	37	81	4
1999–2000	Tier 2	46	22	11	13	65	44	77	5

*Start of Premier League structure

FA Cup

1990–91	1-3 v Brentford (second round)
1991–92	0-3 v Torquay United (first round)
1992–93	0-1 v Reading (first round)
1993–94	1-2 v Kidderminster Harriers (first round)
1994–95	0-0, 1-1 (lost on penalties) v Liverpool (third round)
1995–96	1-1, 1-2 v Wolverhampton Wanderers (third round)
1996–97	1-3 v Wrexham (fifth round)

1997–98   2-3 v Leeds United (fifth round)

1998–99   2-4 v Leicester City (third round)

1999–2000 0-2 v Everton (fourth round)

Football League Cup

1990–91   0-1, 1-1 v Bournemouth (second round, over two legs)

1991–92   1-1, 1-1, 1-2 v Crystal Palace (third round)

1992–93   0-0, 1-4 v Exeter City (first round, over two legs)

1993–94   0-1, 0-1 v Aston Villa (second round, over two legs)

1994–95   0-2, 1-1 v Blackburn Rovers (second round, over two legs)

1995–96   1-2, 0-3 v Leeds United (semi-final, over two legs)

1996–97   1-1, 0-1 v Coventry City (second round, over two legs)

1997–98   1-4 (aet) v Arsenal (third round)

1998–99   1-2 v Wimbledon (third round)

1999–2000 2-3 v West Ham United (fourth round)

21st September 1993

Football League Cup – Second Round

First Leg

Birmingham 0

Aston Villa 1

Richardson

Attendance: 27,815

BIRMINGHAM: *Miller, Hiley, Frain, Parris, Dryden, Whyte, Donowa, Smith, Peschisolido (McMinn), Saville, Shutt*

ASTON VILLA: *Spink (Bosnich), Barrett, Staunton, Teale, McGrath, Richardson, Townsend, Whittingham, Saunders, Cowans, Atkinson*

Goalkeeper Mark Bosnich was the hero for Aston Villa in a dramatic few first-half minutes that killed any hopes of Terry Cooper's side staging an upset.

The Australian had to be brought on as a substitute with 30 minutes gone after Nigel Spink suffered a thigh strain which forced him out of the game.

The game had barely restarted when Dalian Atkinson, back to help out Villa's defence, dived into a clumsy tackle and brought down Andy Saville.

The referee pointed to the spot, to the delight of Blues fans who had waited five years, with their own club lurching from one crisis to another, for another chance to face their biggest rivals.

But defender John Frain, normally a reliable penalty-taker, let nerves get the better of him and Bosnich dived to keep out his shot.

It was a spirited display by City, who had just avoided relegation to the third tier the previous season, and they were denied another penalty when Paul McGrath handled but the ref didn't see it.

Even Villa manager Ron Atkinson admitted his team were lucky, saying: "I thought Paul had forgotten where he was and started playing Gaelic football!"

But if Birmingham felt hard done by over that, they were even more furious when with eight minutes to go a diagonal ball from Steve Staunton reached Kevin Richardson and the Villa skipper applied a calm finish.

"Villa are a quality side but they know they have been in a game," said Blues manager Cooper. "We outplayed them for long periods."

6th October 1993

Football League Cup – Second Round

Second Leg

Aston Villa 1

Saunders

Birmingham 0

Attendance: 35,856

ASTON VILLA: *Bosnich, Cox, Staunton, Teale, McGrath, Richardson, Townsend (Houghton), Daley, Saunders, Cowans, Atkinson*

BIRMINGHAM: *Miller, Hiley (Scott), Frain, Tait, Dryden, Whyte, Donowa (Fenwick), Smith, Mardon, Hooper, Shutt*

Villa manager Ron Atkinson had been delighted when the second-round draw was made in anticipation of two attractive games that would draw big crowds.

In the event he couldn't have known quite how tough the tie against Villa's neighbours would be. While his expensive team – which had been narrowly pipped by Manchester United for the inaugural Premier League title a few months earlier – might never have been in danger of going out, they were still given a tough ride – even against 10 men.

When the Blues had Paul Tait sent off after 64 minutes, most of the crowd expected Villa to exert their superiority, instead they had to wait until the 82nd minute for Dean Saunders to score the goal that guaranteed a place in round three.

Tait was lured into losing his temper when he was caught by a late tackle from Kevin Richardson. The pair squared-up close to the touchline and Tait pushed the Villa captain so hard that he tumbled into the crowd.

Richardson was booked for the tackle, but the retaliation received a more severe punishment.

Manager Terry Cooper went to see Worcestershire referee Gerald Ashby to complain afterwards, claiming: "I have seen a lot worse than that in the Premier League and no action has been taken."

Villa failed to exploit the extra-man advantage, and it needed two good saves by Mark Bosnich to prevent Birmingham's makeshift centre-forward Carl Shutt from bringing the aggregate scores level.

It was a tense and mostly dour affair, but the winning goal had quality – Saunders collected the ball just inside his own half before going on a run which ended with him showing goalkeeper Kevin

Miller a right-footed shot before dragging the ball on to his left and shooting from an acute angle.

It was enough to break Birmingham's resistance, although it would have been cruel if a last-minute goal by Ray Houghton, ruled out for a marginal offside, had been allowed to stand.

The match turned out to have more significance than merely local pride – Atkinson's Villa team went on to lift the trophy after beating Manchester United at Wembley, the club's first silverware since their European Super Cup victory 11 years earlier.

Chapter Ten

The 21st Century

The Premier League and its growing global TV audience changed the face of English football, bringing new challenges to both of Birmingham's big clubs.

Villa had the advantage of being established Premier League members, but even they found increasing difficulty in competing with the financial resources of the clubs backed either by vast global commercial income like Manchester United, or billionaire backers like Chelsea.

John Gregory's team reached the FA Cup final in 2000, losing to Chelsea, but he resigned two years later in frustration at lack of investment to strengthen his side further. Graham Taylor returned but could only finish 16th with a team that lacked stars.

Former Leeds boss David O'Leary's reign began with promise as his team finished sixth, but again it was a false dawn. Ironically when he was given more than £10million to spend on transfer fees in the summer of 2005 it brought the worst season of his three-year reign as his team finished 16th.

Birmingham had come close to a major trophy, meanwhile, with Trevor Francis enduring heartbreak as his side lost a dramatic penalty shoot-out to Liverpool at the Millennium Stadium in the final of the League Cup. A year later, however, they were back at the Millennium in another shoot-out and this time 18-year-old Darren Carter, born in Solihull and brought up through the Blues' youth team, kept his nerve to score the winning spot-kick that took the club back to the elite.

Steve Bruce kept them in the Premier League for four seasons –

but after a bad start in 2007 left to join Wigan, and successor Alex McLeish was unable to prevent a slide back to the Championship. He won promotion at the first attempt, however, and in 2011 landed the first major trophy since 1963 when his side went to Wembley and stunned favourites Arsenal in the League Cup. Sadly the extra games took their toll on a thin squad, and an injury-hit side ended the season back in the relegation zone.

Villa's fortunes during this period were transformed when American billionaire Randy Lerner became owner and appointed Martin O'Neill as his manager. He provided funds for O'Neill to rebuild the side and after finishing 11th in his first season, reached the top six for three campaigns in a row as well as getting to Wembley twice in the League Cup and FA Cup.

The new riches of the biggest clubs were to confound O'Neill's hopes of building a side that could restore their standing from back in the 19th century as regular contenders for major honours, however. He lost star players Gareth Barry and James Milner in successive summers and resigned. It brought a period of turmoil. Former Liverpool manager Gérard Houllier was in charge for a matter of months before being forced to step down through ill health; then the fates of Villa and Birmingham were woven together once more.

After their return to the Premier League, City had been taken over by a Hong Kong-based consortium led by Carson Yeung. Problems emerged when the businessman was charged with money-laundering offences. Following the 2011 relegation McLeish resigned due to difficulties dealing with the owners, and within days was offered the chance to become Villa's next manager. It was a move that was opposed by Villa supporters and led to a difficult season. At least the club survived in the top flight, and did the same – just – under their next manager Paul Lambert, who tried to rebuild recruiting young talent. Birmingham meanwhile just missed out on the play-offs under Chris Hughton, leaving their next boss Lee Clark with the challenge of reviving the club while financial problems went on.

So Villa and Birmingham would have to wait longer for the next time they played against each other in a competitive match. All that will do is stoke up the rivalry all the more for when they meet again.

Record in the 21st Century

Aston Villa:

Season	League	P	W	D	L	F	A	Pts	Position
2000–01	Premier	38	13	15	10	46	43	54	8
2001–02	Premier	38	12	14	12	46	47	50	8
2002–03	Premier	38	12	9	17	42	47	45	16
2003–04	Premier	38	15	11	12	48	44	56	6
2004–05	Premier	38	12	11	15	45	52	47	10
2005–06	Premier	38	10	12	16	42	55	42	16
2006–07	Premier	38	11	17	10	43	41	50	11
2007–08	Premier	38	16	12	10	71	51	60	6
2008–09	Premier	38	17	11	10	54	48	62	6
2009–10	Premier	38	17	13	8	52	39	64	6
2010–11	Premier	38	12	12	14	48	59	48	9
2011–12	Premier	38	7	17	14	37	53	38	16
2012–13	Premier	38	10	11	17	47	69	41	15

FA Cup

2000–01   1-2 v Leicester City (fourth round)

2001–02   2-3 v Manchester United (third round)

2002–03   1-4 v Blackburn Rovers (third round)

2003–04   1-2 v Manchester United (third round)

2004–05   1-3 v Sheffield United (third round)

2005–06   1-1, 1-2 v Manchester City (fifth round)

2006–07   1-2 v Manchester United (third round)

2007–08   0-2 v Manchester United (third round

2008–09   1-3 v Everton (fifth round)

2009–10   0-3 v Chelsea (semi-final)

2010–11	0-3 v Manchester City (fifth round)
2011–12	2-3 v Arsenal (fourth round)
2012–13	1-2 v Millwall (fourth round)

Football League Cup

2000–01	0-1 v Manchester City (second round)
2001–02	0-1 v Sheffield Wednesday (fourth round)
2002–03	3-4 v Liverpool (fifth round)
2003–04	2-5, 2-0 v Bolton Wanderers (semi-final, over two legs)
2004–05	1-3 v Burnley (third round)
2005–06	0-3 v Doncaster Rovers (fourth round)
2006–07	0-4 v Chelsea (fourth round)
2007–08	0-1 v Leicester City (third round)
2008–09	0-1 v Queens Park Rangers (third round)
2009–10	1-2 v Manchester United (final at Wembley Stadium)
2010–11	1-2 v Birmingham (fifth round)
2011–12	0-2 v Bolton Wanderers (third round)
2012–13	1-3, 2-1 v Bradford City (semi-final, over two legs)

European Competition

2000–01	did not qualify
2001–02	UEFA Cup 2-3, 1-0 v NK Varteks
2002–03	did not qualify
2003–04	did not qualify
2004–05	did not qualify
2005–06	did not qualify
2006–07	did not qualify
2007–08	did not qualify
2008–09	UEFA Cup 1-1, 0-2 v CSKA Moscow (first knock-out round)
2009–10	UEFA Cup 0-1, 2-1 v Rapid Vienna (first qualifying round, lost on away goal
2010–11	UEFA Cup 1-1, 2-3 v Rapid Vienna (first qualifying round)

| 2011–12 | did not qualify |
| 2012–13 | did not qualify |

Birmingham:

Season	League	P	W	D	L	F	A	Pts	Position
2000–01	Tier 2	46	23	9	14	59	48	78	5
2001–02	Tier 2	46	21	13	12	70	49	76	5
2002–03	Premier	38	13	9	16	41	49	48	13
2003–04	Premier	38	12	14	12	43	48	50	10
2004–05	Premier	38	11	12	15	40	46	45	12
2005–06	Premier	38	8	10	20	28	50	34	18
2006–07	Tier 2	46	26	8	12	67	42	86	2
2007–08	Premier	38	8	11	19	46	62	35	19
2008–09	Tier 2	46	23	14	9	54	37	83	2
2009–10	Premier	38	13	11	14	38	47	50	9
2010–11	Premier	38	8	15	15	37	58	39	18
2011–12	Tier 2	46	20	16	10	78	51	76	4
2012–13	Tier 2	46	15	16	15	63	69	61	12

FA Cup

2000–01	2-3 v Manchester City (third round)
2001–02	0-3 v Liverpool (third round)
2002–03	1-3 v Fulham (third round)
2003–04	1-1, 0-2 v Sunderland (fifth round)
2004–05	0-2 v Chelsea (fourth round)
2005–06	0-7 v Liverpool (sixth round)
2006–07	2-3 v Reading (fourth round)
2007–08	1-2 v Huddersfield (third round)
2008–09	0-2 v Wolverhampton Wanderers (third round)
2009–10	0-2 v Portsmouth (sixth round)
2010–11	2-3 v Bolton Wanderers (sixth round)
2011–12	1-1, 0-2 v Chelsea (fifth round)
2012–13	1-1, 1-2 v Leeds United (third round)

Football League Cup

2000–01	1-1, lost 4-5 on penalties v Liverpool (final at Millennium Stadium)
2001–02	0-6 v Manchester City (third round)
2002–03	0-2 v Preston North End (third round)
2003–04	0-1 v Blackpool (second round)
2004–05	0-1 v Fulham (third round)
2005–06	1-3 v Manchester United (fifth round)
2006–07	0-1 v Liverpool (fourth round)
2007–08	0-3 v Blackburn Rovers (third round)
2008–09	0-2 v Southampton (second round)
2009–10	0-2 v Sunderland (third round)
2010–11	2-1 v Arsenal (final at Wembley)
2011–12	0-2 v Manchester City (third round)
2012–13	2-3 v Coventry (second round)

European Competition

2011–12	Europa League finished third in Group H

16th September 2002

Premier League

Birmingham 3

Morrison, Enckelman (og), Horsfield

Aston Villa 0

Attendance 29,505

BIRMINGHAM: *Vaesen, Kenna, Purse, Cunningham, Grainger, Devlin, Savage (Hughes), Cissé, D. Johnson, John, Morrison (Horsfield)*

ASTON VILLA: *Enckelman, Mellberg, Alpay, Staunton, Samuel, de la Cruz, Kinsella, Johnsen, Barry, Allback (Vassell), Ángel (Dublin)*

This is the game that will always be remembered for Peter Enckelman's bizarre own goal that handed Birmingham victory.

It was a goal that will always be debated. City had taken a first-half lead through Clinton Morrison, but were standing firm against an onslaught by the visiting team as the clock ticked into the final 15 minutes of the game.

Villa defender Olof Mellberg took a throw-in in his own half, and propelled the ball back towards his goalkeeper, only for Enckelman to let the ball run underneath his foot and into the goal.

The Finnish keeper immediately threw up his hands in horror, and maybe that made up referee David Elleray's mind that he had touched the ball as it went under his foot.

Elleray, more than 30 yards away, insisted later that he'd seen a touch but video evidence suggested it might not have happened – which would have made it only a corner and not a goal – and Villa defender Steve Staunton was booked for protesting about the decision.

Manager Graham Taylor was also angry afterwards, insisting that Elleray couldn't possibly have been certain enough there had been a touch to award the goal.

And in the pandemonium that followed, a Blues fan ran onto the pitch and taunted the goalkeeper, who very calmly ignored the provocation.

Six minutes later all the arguments were academic as Villa's Turkish defender Alpay made an error that handed possession to Blues substitute Geoff Horsfield who took the chance to make it 3-0.

Villa fans will always claim they were hard done by over a goal that shouldn't have been given – Blues supporters will always say that their side was winning anyway and were feeding on the passionate atmosphere of the home crowd.

Certainly Villa's players struggled for a while to deal with the occasion. Morrison's goal came when Mellberg fluffed an attempted clearance and Robbie Savage was quickest to react.

Savage's energy, running and tackling in midfield played a crucial role – though he and Dion Dublin were both booked after a second-half clash. There would be more problems between the pair later that season.

3rd March 2003

Premier League
Aston Villa 0
Birmingham 2
Lazaridis, Horsfield
Attendance: **42,602**
ASTON VILLA: *Enckelman, Samuel, Johnsen, Mellberg, Wright (Crouch), Gudjonsson, Hendrie, Barry, Vassell, Dublin, Moore (Hadji)*
BIRMINGHAM: *Vaesen, Kenna, Cunningham, Upson, Clapham, D. Johnson, Savage (Carter), Clemence, Lazaridis (Devlin) Dugarry, Morrison (Horsfield)*

If the derby back in October had been spiky, this one was downright spiteful, played in a brooding and angry atmosphere of confrontations between supporters and nasty clashes on the field, too.

It came to a head five minutes after the interval when Robbie Savage was caught by a tackle from Dion Dublin. Several players crowded round as referee Mark Halsey awarded the free kick, and then Dublin clearly head-butted the Birmingham man.

Halsey had no option but to produce his red card, Savage clutched his face, and as he walked towards the tunnel the big Villa centre-forward could be seen mouthing "he's a cheat" into a TV camera.

That wasn't the end of the home team's disciplinary problems on a night when they were so stoked-up by manager Graham Taylor in search of revenge for the defeat at St Andrew's earlier in the season, that they completely lost their composure.

A series of bad tackles and running feuds all over the pitch ended in Icelandic midfielder Joey Gudjonsson diving into a horrible two-footed lunge at Matthew Upson 10 minutes from time and he also saw red.

By then the match was effectively over anyway, as Birmingham had taken a two goal lead against 10 men, and nine were never going to mount a comeback.

The first goal came when Jeff Kenna got away from Alan Wright on the right touchline, and sent in a cross that found Stan Lazaridis unmarked at the far post.

Then Villa goalkeeper Peter Enckelman, who had spent the season rebuilding his confidence following the debacle of the St Andrew's derby, buckled in the poisonous atmosphere and made another error.

Jlloyd Samuel's back-header should have been easy for him to gather, but as Geoff Horsfield chased him down, the goalkeeper ducked the challenge and allowed the forward to poke the ball free and stroke it into an empty net.

Enckelman, not for the first time that season, sank to his knees in despair as the visiting fans celebrated.

The truth of the game, though, was that Villa had again been the architects of their own downfall. In a poor performance they produced only one meaningful attempt on goal, when Gudjonsson's free-kick went over the bar, even before they were down to 10 men.

19th October 2003

Premier League
Birmingham 0
Aston Villa 0
Attendance: 29,546
BIRMINGHAM: *Bennett, Clapham, Cunningham, Upson, Johnson (Tébily), Lazaridis (Cissé), Clemence, Savage, Dunn, Forssell, Dugarry (Morrison)*
ASTON VILLA: *Sorensen, Delaney, Johnsen, Mellberg, Samuel, de la Cruz, Hendrie (Whittingham), McCann, Barry, Vassell, Ángel*

After the troubles of the previous season, the game was moved to a midday kick-off on police advice. But in the event this was the High Noon derby which turned into anything but a gunfight.

Maybe it was because Aston Villa's new manager David O'Leary had seen the rancour that had followed for his predecessor Graham Taylor after the previous year's two defeats and wanted to play safe; for whatever the reason it was a game that drifted into a stalemate.

O'Leary had been forced to deal with an added disciplinary issue in the build-up to the game – his Turkish defender Alpay had been involved in a tunnel confrontation with David Beckham the previous weekend when both were on international duty.

Alpay had been roundly condemned for his part in the problems, and O'Leary, aware of the hothouse atmosphere he could expect at St Andrew's in any case, left the defender out of his team to try to keep tempers calmed.

In general, after the ugly scenes of the previous season, this was a well-ordered affair with Mike Riley the referee doing well to keep things cool.

Birmingham had made an impressive start to the season and were sat in fourth place in the table going into the game. As their manager Steve Bruce said afterwards: "It is a measure of how far we have come that we are sat in the dressing room full of disappointment that we have not won the game."

The nearest they came was a first-half opportunity that Stephen Clemence wasted – while Villa also missed a good opportunity to snatch all three points late in the game as youngster Peter Whittingham got clear but lifted his shot over the bar.

O'Leary insisted afterwards that he had brought his team across the city with the intention of winning rather than just settling for a point. But the whole match was more about fear of losing on both sides, rather than a desire for victory.

22ⁿᵈ February 2004

Premier League

Aston Villa 2

Vassell, Hitzlsperger

Birmingham 2

Forssell, John

Attendance: **40,061**

ASTON VILLA: *Sorensen, de la Cruz, Mellberg, Johnsen (Dublin), Samuel, Hendrie (L. Moore), Solano, Hitzlsperger, Barry (Whittingham), Vassell, Ángel*

BIRMINGHAM: *Maik Taylor, Tébily, Cunningham, Purse, Kenna (John), Johnson, Clemence (Morrison), Savage, Hughes, Dugarry (Dunn), Forssell*

After a slow start to the season under David O'Leary, his team were just beginning to hit some form when City arrived at Villa Park.

They had won their three previous League games – scoring five against Leicester – and the mood of confidence was reflected in the way they started the game.

They hit the woodwork inside 10 minutes with Nobby Solano's free kick just deflected off Darren Purse to avoid a certain goal, and then Thomas Hitzlsperger tried a shot from outside the box that flashed narrowly wide.

With Gareth Barry dominating midfield from the left, the pressure on Birmingham's defence was growing, and they cracked after 21 minutes when inevitably it was Barry who set up Darius Vassell for a simple tap-in from three yards.

Vassell missed two good chances before the break – but within two minutes of the restart his pace had unsettled the Blues again and the ball fell for Hitzlsperger to strike a spectacular 20-yard shot that gave Maik Taylor no chance.

Juan Pablo Ángel missed another opportunity – but then completely against the run of play, City broke away to pull a goal back.

Robbie Savage, so often the central figure in derbies at this time, was involved in a breakaway attack before Clinton Morrison held off a Dion Dublin challenge to set up Mikael Forssell to finish.

Villa claimed the ball had gone out for a throw-in that wasn't awarded in the build-up, and somehow in their frustration allowed the momentum to change.

Goalkeeper Sorensen saved well to stop Morrison equalizing, and it seemed that might be enough for the home side to cling on for the victory.

But with four minutes of stoppage time played Morrison found space again, and Sorensen could only push his shot into the path of substitute Stern John who gleefully grabbed the equalizer.

It was a comeback that had a significant effect on Birmingham as they established themselves under Steve Bruce in their second season in the Premier League.

They won their next two games, and went on to record a top-10 finish, the club's highest League position at the end of a season since 1973.

12th December 2004

Premier League

Aston Villa 1

Barry

Birmingham 2

Morrison, Dunn

Attendance: 41,329

ASTON VILLA: *Sorensen, de la Cruz, Delaney, Mellberg, Samuel, Solano, McCann, Davis, Barry, Cole, Ángel*

BIRMINGHAM: *Maik Taylor, Tébily, Upson, Cunningham, Lazaridis (Clapham), Johnson, Carter, Savage, Dunn (Gray), Morrison (Anderton), Heskey*

All the bitter rivalry between the two clubs was stoked up by Villa skipper Olof Mellberg in the week before the game when he gave an interview slating Birmingham and saying he could never play for the club.

Birmingham City boss Steve Bruce responded by posting the newspaper cuttings around his dressing room and his side came out fired-up to do their talking on the pitch.

Nine minutes into the game Thomas Sorensen became the latest victim of the "goalkeeper's curse" that seems to have always settled on the second city derby when he fumbled a harmless-looking shot from Clinton Morrison and let the ball squirm across the line into the goal.

Villa, who had not lost at home all season, were suddenly drained of confidence and the Blues sensed the chance to go for the jugular.

They duly doubled their lead when Damien Johnson's cross picked out David Dunn and he finished calmly.

Villa were second-best all over the pitch. Even when they did get the ball in the net Gareth Barry had used his hand, Diego Maradona-style, to flick on a free-kick at the near post and he was booked by referee Steve Dunn.

Again it was Savage who was the pantomime villain for the home fans, snapping into tackles. But that made him the hero for the visitors as he dominated midfield.

The Blues settled for slowing the game and controlling their lead in the second half, and by the time Barry got a goal in the final minute it was far too late to make a difference to the result.

Birmingham boss Bruce couldn't resist a dig back at Mellberg afterwards. "I just let his comments float around our dressing room, with all this rubbish about how he would never play for Birmingham.

"Let me tell you that after that performance he would never get a game for us, because Kenny Cunningham and Matthew Upson are far, far better."

20th March 2005

Premier League

Birmingham 2

Heskey, Gray

Aston Villa 0

Attendance: 29,382

BIRMINGHAM: *Maik Taylor, Melchiot, Cunningham, Upson, Clapham, Johnson, Carter, Clemence (Nafti), Lazaridis (Gray), Pandiani (Morrison), Heskey*

ASTON VILLA: *Sorensen, de la Cruz, Mellberg, Laursen, Samuel, Solano (Hitzlsperger), Hendrie, Berson (Vassell), Davis, Barry, Moore (Cole)*

Maybe Thomas Sorensen was still having nightmares about his error in the Villa Park game earlier this season – but whatever the reason, the derby curse came back to afflict him again.

Villa's Danish international keeper, so consistent throughout a campaign in which an average team still managed to finish in the top half of the table, came up with another blunder to hand the game to the Blues all gift-wrapped.

Birmingham had been in a bad run, losing seven of their previous nine League games, and were grateful for their good fortune.

"My players owed the supporters something, and they responded to the challenge," said delighted manager Steve Bruce afterwards. "We had some luck, but derby games are often decided by individual mistakes."

There had been little in the game in the first half – apart from a Nolberto Solano free-kick that Maik Taylor had tipped onto the post – and in the interval it looked as if a 0-0 draw was the most likely outcome.

But then two minutes after the break Emile Heskey shrugged off Martin Laursen's challenge and worked the ball wide of Olof Mellberg to hit a shot that shouldn't have caused any real danger.

Instead Sorensen allowed it to squirm under his body at the

near post, and was left lying on his back staring forlornly at the sky as the home stands at St Andrew's rocked in celebration.

He recovered to make an excellent save soon afterwards from Walter Pandiani, but the damage had been done on a day when Birmingham's defenders Kenny Cunningham and Matthew Upson were again in magnificent form.

In fact home goalkeeper Maik Taylor wasn't even tested until a late shot by Villa substitute Thomas Hitzlsperger. Not long afterwards substitute Julian Gray took advantage of hesitant Villa defending to get the second goal that wrapped up Blues' second double over their big rivals in three years.

Villa boss David O'Leary admitted: "Birmingham seem to have a hoodoo on us. They must love playing against us, because we gave away stupid goals.

"They did not do much to outplay us, but individual mistakes were costly. Everyone is very quiet in our dressing room."

16th October 2005

Premier League
Birmingham 0
Aston Villa 1
Phillips
Attendance: 29,312

BIRMINGHAM: *Maik Taylor, Tébily, Martin Taylor, Upson, Clapham (Dunn), Pennant, Johnson, Clemence (Jarošik), Gray, Heskey, Pandiani (Forssell)*

ASTON VILLA: *Sorensen, Hughes, Mellberg, Ridgewell, Bouma, Milner, Davis, Bakke (Djemba-Djemba), Barry (Berger), Moore, Phillips (Ángel)*

David O'Leary was under pressure after one win in eight games. News had leaked out that Villa chairman Doug Ellis had begun talks about selling the club, the crowd were calling for the Irishman to lose his job, and the pressure was on.

Maybe that explains O'Leary's wild reaction at the final whistle after a Kevin Phillips goal had finally brought his club a Premier League victory over their nearest and most bitter rivals.

He ran across the pitch, repeatedly punching the air in the direction of the directors' box – a gesture that inflamed the home fans.

But he insisted afterwards: "I just wanted to show the chairman how pleased I was for him – he has been ill and he made a big effort to come today."

It was Villa's first away win in six months, created by a performance that showed far more energy and passion than in previous games.

They deserved to be rewarded after 19 minutes when James Milner's pass to Gareth Barry opened up the home defence, and he picked out Phillips' run with a clever back-heel.

The striker who had once won the Golden Boot in his Sunderland days had been out for a month with a calf injury, but was razor-sharp as he struck a low shot from the edge of the area into the bottom left-hand corner.

Birmingham dominated the possession in the second half, but without ever really breaking down a Villa defence which showed far more determination.

In young Northern Ireland midfielder Steven Davis Villa had the game's outstanding player, working to break up the visitors' momentum.

Most pleasing of all for the visitors, though, was the composed performance of goalkeeper Thomas Sorensen who shut out constant taunts from the home fans over his howlers in the previous season to keep a clean sheet for only the second time in this campaign.

"He deserves big credit," said O'Leary. "There was a little rumour going around the place about whether he would fancy facing it today, and he stood up superbly."

For Birmingham the consequences were dire. "It's going to be a long hard winter and it will definitely be a scrap," admitted Steve Bruce. They slipped into the bottom three when Fulham drew at Charlton the following night, and that set the tone for a campaign that ultimately ended in relegation – but only after their rivals had pushed them closer to the edge.

16ᵗʰ April 2006

Premier League

Aston Villa 3

Baroš (2), Cahill

Birmingham 1

Sutton

Attendance: 40,158

ASTON VILLA: *Sorensen, Hughes, Ridgewell, Cahill, Samuel, Milner (Agbonlahor), McCann, Davis (Gardner), Barry, Baroš, Phillips (Ángel)*

BIRMINGHAM: *Maik Taylor, Tébily, Cunningham (Lazaridis), Sadler, Martin Taylor, Pennant, Butt, Johnson, Dunn (Forssell), Heskey, Sutton*

Youth team product Gary Cahill made himself an instant hero with Aston Villa fans as he scored a spectacular scissor-kick in only his second Premier League start.

A tense contest had seen Chris Sutton wipe out an early goal by Milan Baroš and home nerves were beginning to jangle before Villa won a corner.

As the ball fell loose, Cahill swivelled acrobatically in mid-air and smashed it past Birmingham keeper Maik Taylor, before earning a booking for his celebrations. He admitted afterwards: "I didn't know much about it. I just saw the ball in the air, I jumped up and swung my foot. It is not the sort of thing I do very regularly. I did get one for Burnley while I was on loan, but that was a tap-in from a yard out. This one was a bit more special, with all the circumstances of the game and it being in front of the home fans. I won't forget it in a hurry. I wanted to have a look at it again so one of the Villa

Park staff showed it to me on their laptop. It is just tremendous, a dream come true. We wanted to show we are the biggest club in the Midlands and we've done it."

The result effectively condemned Birmingham to relegation four seasons after Steve Bruce had won promotion through the play-offs.

Yet they had shown great character after falling behind in 10 minutes when Gavin McCann's superb cross-field ball fell to James Milner who set up Aaron Hughes to cross for Baroš to fire home.

They equalized quickly as Kenny Cunningham's free-kick found Chris Sutton who fired home his first Birmingham goal, and the momentum stayed with them but they were unable to find a finishing touch against Cahill and Liam Ridgewell who had played together in the youth team.

After Nicky Butt was injured in a collision with Kevin Phillips, they began losing ground in midfield.

After Cahill's goal there was no way back and Villa could sense blood. With space opening up Baroš was in his element and his second came thanks to fine work from Milner and sub Juan Pablo Ángel.

11th November 2007

Premier League
Birmingham 1
Forssell
Aston Villa 2
Ridgewell (og), Agbonlahor
Attendance: 26,539
BIRMINGHAM: *Taylor, Kelly, Djourou, Ridgewell, Schmitz, de Ridder, Nafti (Larsson), Muamba, Kapo, Palacios (Forssell), Jerome (O'Connor)*
ASTON VILLA: *Carson, Mellberg, Laursen, Knight, Bouma, Reo-Coker, Petrov, Barry, Young, Carew (Moore), Agbonlahor*

For Villa fan and player Gabby Agbonlahor it was a dream ending to a derby – for former Villa player Liam Ridgewell it was a nightmare.

With a couple of minutes to go striker Agbonlahor first cleared off his line from a header by Ridgewell, and then went straight up the other end of the pitch to score the winner.

Ironically the two of them were big mates from the time they both came together through the youth ranks at Villa's Bodymoor Heath Academy.

But it left Ridgewell admitting: "I went up to Gabby and swore at him at the end, I can't believe the way the game finished."

It had started badly for the £2million defender as well. With just nine minutes gone he tried to deal with a Stiliyan Petrov cross but only succeeded in deflecting it past his own goalkeeper Maik Taylor.

Visiting fans who had started by jeering his name began an ironic chorus of "there's only one Liam Ridgewell".

And there wasn't too much sympathy afterwards, either, from his former manager Martin O'Neill.

"I wish he had put in another four", he said.

City thought they should have had two first-half penalties. First defender Zat Knight appeared to handle, and then referee Steve Bennett booked Blues star Daniël de Ridder for diving even though Martin Laursen appeared to catch his ankle in the box.

Birmingham manager Steve Bruce fumed: "How the referee misses the first one I don't know because we have all seen it bar him. As for the second one, de Ridder said at half-time he was caught and, having seen it on TV, it was blatant.

"I am not saying we would have won the game but it would have put us in a strong position if we had got two penalties."

Instead he brought on substitute Mikael Forssell who headed home a 62nd-minute equalizer from de Ridder's right-wing cross.

That stirred Birmingham's fans into life and Cameron Jerome almost fired the Blues in front but Villa keeper Scott Carson made a brilliant save.

But the real drama was saved for the closing minutes as Agbonlahor made a vital goal-line clearance from Ridgewell's header at Sebastian Larsson's corner before popping up to head in Ashley Young's cross in the 87th minute in front of the ecstatic away fans.

20th April 2008

Premier League

Aston Villa 5

A. Young (2), Carew (2), Agbonlahor

Birmingham 1

Forssell

Attendance: 42,584

ASTON VILLA: *Carson, Mellberg (Harewood), Laursen, Knight, Bouma, A. Young, Reo-Coker, Petrov, Barry, Carew, Agbonlahor*

BIRMINGHAM: *Taylor, Kelly, Jaïdi, Ridgewell, Murphy, Jerome (Kapo), Nafti, Muamba, McSheffrey, Zárate (Forssell), McFadden*

Villa were on the crest of a Martin O'Neill-inspired wave and trying to take fifth place to earn entry to Europe – Birmingham were battling to avoid the drop after Alex McLeish had taken over from Steve Bruce midway through the season.

In the event both sides missed out, with Blues going down to the Championship and Villa having to settle for sixth place in a freak year where that didn't qualify for Continental competition.

Ashley Young and John Carew both scored twice to lead the way in a five-goal mauling that was the biggest margin in a second city derby since Villa had also scored five in a League Cup tie 20 years earlier.

The writing was on the wall from early in the game, even though Blues started brightly. The home midfield of Stiliyan Petrov and Gareth Barry began to dominate the game, and the breakthrough came in the 28th minute when Young smashed in an unstoppable right-foot shot from just inside the area following a mishit attempt by Olof Mellberg.

The hosts then took a stranglehold on the game when Carew

headed in from Young's free-kick in the 42nd minute.

Villa's superiority was just embarrassing after the break as Barry unselfishly laid on a second for Norway star Carew to make it 3-0.

Brum boss Alex McLeish responded by replacing Mauro Zárate with top scorer Mikael Forssell, and Scotland striker James McFadden missed a free header before Young got on the scoresheet again in the 63rd minute.

Despite Forssell pulling a goal back on 67 minutes, many Blues fans had by then left in disgust. There was still time for Gabby Agbonlahor to notch in the 78th minute with a low right-foot finish from outside the box.

Villa, who had beaten Bolton 4-0 and Derby 6-0 in their previous two games, were playing with a rich vein of confidence and even McLeish admitted: "Villa played fantastically and their front men caused havoc.

"People like John Carew were unplayable and they are miles away from us at the moment."

13th September 2009

Premier League

Birmingham 0

Aston Villa 1

Agbonlahor

Attendance: **25,196**

BIRMINGHAM: *Hart, Parnaby, Johnson, Queudrue, Tainio, Larsson, Ferguson, Bowyer, McFadden (Carsley, Phillips), Fahey, O'Connor (Benítez)*

ASTON VILLA: *Friedel, Cuellar, Dunne, Collins, Warnock, Milner, Sidwell, Reo-Coker (Carew), Petrov, A. Young, Agbonlahor*

Aston Villa manager Martin O'Neill had spent nearly £20million a fortnight earlier signing three new defenders – but international matches meant his new unit had barely been able to train together.

Even so, the fresh faces of Richard Dunne, James Collins and Stephen Warnock quickly blended with Carlos Cuellar to ensure that goalkeeper Brad Friedel had a relatively comfortable afternoon.

It was the first look at a back four that would go on to have a hugely successful season for O'Neill, taking Villa to Wembley twice.

The manager said: "I was very pleased with all three new signings. Without exerting an incredible amount of pressure on Birmingham, we were reasonably comfortable.

"That is a tribute to the new players, who only had Friday and Saturday to acquaint themselves with one another."

O'Neill's side ultimately won the game with a goal five minutes from the end as Gabby Agbonlahor found some room after substitute John Carew had headed an Ashley Young free-kick back into the danger area.

Agbonlahor had been suffering abuse from Blues fans throughout the game but in a week when Emmanuel Adebayor had been in trouble for gesturing to abusive Arsenal supporters, he found a better way to answer them back.

Two seasons earlier he had also scored a late winner at St Andrew's, and he said: "I thought about what happened, then, looked up at the clock and thought it would be a good time to do the same again – then the chance came.

"Our fans were brilliant – they inspired me. Whenever they sing the song about me, the Birmingham fans repeat it with different words, and that makes me even more determined to do well."

There were nearly 5,000 empty seats for the midday kick off, a response to prices which had been raised to £48 a seat.

Though Birmingham worked hard there was only one occasion, when Lee Bowyer burst clear only to see his shot parried by Brad Friedel, on which they seriously threatened to score.

Not that Villa were all that more threatening – it was 12 minutes from time before Joe Hart had to make a proper save to keep out Steve Sidwell's header.

25th April 2010

Premier League

Aston Villa 1

Milner (pen)

Birmingham 0

Attendance: 42,788

ASTON VILLA: *Friedel, Cuellar, Dunne, Collins, Warnock, Petrov, Young, Milner, Downing, Carew (Heskey), Agbonlahor*

BIRMINGHAM: *Hart, Carr, Johnson, Ridgewell, Vignal (Parnaby), Larsson (Fahey), Gardner (Phillips), Bowyer, Ferguson, McFadden, Jerome*

Villa's third win in a week made sure they would finish sixth and qualify for Europe – but Birmingham raged with a sense of injustice over the late penalty decision which decided the game.

Gabby Agbonlahor went down after being challenged in the box by Roger Johnson. TV replays suggested the Birmingham defender had got the ball but referee Martin Atkinson gave the penalty and James Milner scored – despite the efforts of his former England Under-21 team-mate Joe Hart to put him off by trying to stare him out.

Johnson was still angry afterwards, insisting: "I got the ball cleanly, everyone could see that, and the ref can't make a decision if he's not sure.

"The rules say if you're not sure, you don't give a penalty. Villa are at home, they've got the crowd behind them, and the ref has made a split second decision which is plain wrong."

It was actually Villa's goalkeeper who had the biggest say in the game. A month before his 39th birthday, American Brad Friedel was in superb form.

One second-half save from Cameron Jerome – with his face – was as brave as it was brilliant, and on the rare occasions he was beaten, Carlos Cuellar and Stewart Downing came to the rescue with goal-line clearances.

Villa looked tired during the game as they came towards the end of a mammoth season in which they had been to Wembley for both a League Cup final and an FA Cup semi-final.

Birmingham's best chances in the first half of a slow-burner fell to Sebastian Larsson. As early as the ninth minute, he skipped round Friedel only to shank his finish, from a tight angle, horribly into the Holte End.

When Richard Dunne inexplicably missed Friedel's bowling-green clearance, Larsson was too startled to capitalize.

Villa had their moments, notably when Hart tipped over James Collins' fierce volley, but their threat was only sporadic where the Blues' application was relentless.

Milner's cool finish from the spot ultimately meant that Villa extended their run to six derby victories in a row.

Manager Martin O'Neill insisted his team deserved any fortune. He said: "I've only seen one slow-motion replay and I thought it looked a clear penalty.

"Birmingham might feel aggrieved but big decisions went against us on our two trips to Wembley this season."

31st October 2010

Premier League
Aston Villa 0
Birmingham 0
Attendance: 40,468
ASTON VILLA: *Friedel, L. Young, Collins, Dunne, Warnock, Reo-Coker (Carew), Clark, Sidwell (Bannan), A. Young, Heskey, Downing*
BIRMINGHAM: *Foster, Carr, Johnson, Dann, Ridgewell, Larsson, Gardner, Ferguson, Fahey, Hleb (Jerome), Žigić*

Referee Howard Webb was the central figure in a game that was tense and sometimes bad-tempered, but ultimately ended in stalemate.

Villa skipper Nigel Reo-Coker was fortunate not to be sent off for kicking out at old team-mate Craig Gardner. The two of them clashed twice but both got only yellow cards – even though each time the exchanges provoked other players into joining in.

Both managers hinted afterwards that the two players held a grudge from their time together at Villa Park.

Frenchman Houllier picked a negative side in response to injury problems that had left him without another striker to support Emile Heskey.

Keith Fahey, another ex-Villa man, managed to fire in three different first-half efforts – two of which tested keeper Brad Friedel.

Birmingham also had a penalty appeal before the break when Reo-Coker appeared to handle the ball in the box. It was a massive let-off for the home side as the incident was near referee Howard Webb.

But Birmingham were lucky themselves when Nikola Žigić escaped a red card for catching James Collins with an elbow before the break.

Villa had to wait until the 70th minute for their first corner which Collins headed harmlessly wide.

Gardner and Reo-Coker then clashed again when the Villa man went in the book after kicking out at his ex-team-mate.

The bust-up seemed to inspire Villa as Clark headed just wide in the closing minutes and Ashley Young hit the post late on.

But ultimately it was the refereeing decisions which provided the only talking points from a dire contest, which meant Villa had gone 344 minutes without a goal in the Premier League.

1st December 2010

Football League Cup Quarter-Final

Birmingham 2

Larsson (pen), Žigić

Aston Villa 1

Agbonlahor

Attendance: 27,679

BIRMINGHAM: *Foster, Carr, Johnson, Dann, Ridgewell, Larsson (Murphy), Ferguson, Bowyer (Gardner), Fahey, Jerome, Žigić (Derbyshire)*
ASTON VILLA: *Friedel, L. Young, Dunne, Collins, Warnock (Pires), A. Young, Clark, Hogg (Delfouneso), Bannan (Ireland), Downing, Agbonlahor*

For the first time since the ugly scenes that marked the derbies in the 2002–03 season, the authorities allowed City and Villa to meet in a night game, but it ended in more crowd trouble.

Nikola Žigić's header six minutes from the end deflected off defender James Collins for the winning goal which set up Birmingham for a semi-final against West Ham.

But at the final whistle, delighted home fans poured on to the pitch to celebrate the victory and many then ran to the visiting section to goad Villa fans about their first win against their big rivals in eight attempts.

A police cordon kept them apart, but when missiles were thrown the trouble escalated and it took a baton charge by police to bring it to an end.

With live TV cameras showing the scenes, it was a poor signal to send to the world the night before FIFA were due to vote on England's bid to be the host country for the 2018 World Cup.

Even manager Alex McLeish admitted: "It was pretty horrible to see punters on the pitch – we don't condone that behaviour, it's a return to the dark ages.

"I know we hadn't beaten Villa for a long time, and our fans were treating it like a Cup final, which is fair enough.

"But when you see flares being thrown into the crowd, it's not something you want to be associated with.

"It would have been nice if my players had been able to celebrate reaching a semi-final by giving our supporters a wave from the middle."

Villa showed character to equalize when Gabriel Agbonlahor's

30th-minute goal cancelled out a Sebastian Larsson penalty, awarded by referee Chris Foy after Lee Bowyer was fouled from behind by Richard Dunne.

Seconds earlier Blues had an effort controversially ruled out for offside when Žigić's shot squirmed over the line.

It was the third successive game at St Andrew's in which Villa fan Agbonlahor had scored, and Villa then dominated the second half but found Birmingham keeper Ben Foster in good form as he made a double save from Stephen Ireland and Ashley Young.

That set up the finish and giant striker Žigić scored the winner from Cameron Jerome's cross.

16th January 2011

Premier League
Birmingham 1
Johnson
Aston Villa 1
Collins
Attendance: 22,287
BIRMINGHAM: *Foster, Carr, Johnson, Ridgewell, Murphy, Bentley, Gardner, Ferguson, Fahey, Hleb (Žigić), Derbyshire (Bowyer)*
ASTON VILLA: *Friedel, Walker, Collins, Dunne, Clark, Albrighton, Petrov, Reo-Coker (Bannan), Downing, Carew (Delfouneso), Agbonlahor*

Defender James Collins scored with a deflected shot 17 minutes from the end to take a point for Villa which dragged them out of the relegation zone on goal difference.

It was a crucial result for manager Gérard Houllier who had been under pressure following a 1-0 home defeat by Sunderland which had followed thrashings at Manchester City and Liverpool.

At this stage of the season it was Birmingham who were definitely top dogs in the city, having knocked Villa out of the Carling Cup a month earlier.

Alex McLeish's side were to go on and win that competition – the club's first major trophy since the League Cup was in its infancy in 1963. But what nobody knew after the final whistle blew at St Andrew's on this Sunday afternoon was that it would end up being City, rather than Villa, who finished in the bottom three.

In fact McLeish, ironically later to take over from Frenchman Houllier as Villa's manager, hailed the game as a turning point in ending Aston Villa's domination of the contest between the two clubs.

He said: "We've come a long way in a couple of years in terms of these games and the results. Had we been a wee bit more clinical we would have seen it through.

"When it was 1-0 we really had to turn the screw but Villa came back into it.

"I felt we played some really good football. Collins' shot wasn't even on target, it hit one of our defenders and went in."

David Bentley, on loan from Tottenham, was the man-of-the-match with a creative performance in midfield that caused problems for a Villa side missing Emile Heskey and Ashley Young through suspension.

They fell behind after 49 minutes when defender Roger Johnson was quickest to react to a loose ball in the box after Craig Gardner's powerful shot was blocked. Goalkeeper Brad Friedel then produced an important save from Matt Derbyshire.

Villa had been heavily criticized by fans for their lack of fight in the previous defeats, but they found some character and had got back into the game even before Collins equalized – they actually hit the woodwork four times in all.

Collins said: "We put in a battling performance and it can really kick us on.

"No one is happy with the way we have been performing. It is down to the players to really dig in and hopefully the spirit we showed will spur us on.

"When you are down there the one thing you need to show is fight and commitment and we certainly did that today."

ASTON VILLA vs BIRMINGHAM CITY